Beverly Carradine

Heart Talks

Beverly Carradine

Heart Talks

ISBN/EAN: 9783744724319

Printed in Europe, USA, Canada, Australia, Japan

Cover: Foto ©Thomas Meinert / pixelio.de

More available books at **www.hansebooks.com**

HEART TALKS

BY

REV. B. CARRADINE, D. D.

AUTHOR OF

Sanctification—A Journey to Palestine—The Second Blessing in Symbol—The Lottery Exposed—The Bottle—Church Entertainments—The Better Way—The Old Man—Pastoral Sketches—The Sanctified Life—And Revival Sermons.

M. W. KNAPP,
PUBLISHER OF GOSPEL LITERATURE.
REVIVALIST OFFICE, CINCINNATI, OHIO.
Copyrighted 1899 by M. W. Knapp.

CONTENTS.

		PAGE.
I.	My Conversion,	3
II.	Call to the Ministry,	12
III.	My Sanctification,	25
IV.	Call to the Evangelistic Work,	37
V.	Revivals,	47
VI.	Altar Work,	56
VII.	The Secret of the Lord,	69
VIII.	Without Reputation,	77
IX.	The Comfort in Temptation,	88
X.	The Four Looks Toward Sodom,	98
XI.	The Strength of Samson,	106
XII.	The Defeat at Ai,	117
XIII.	The Sifter and Fan,	126
XIV.	The Battle is not Yours,	134
XV.	The Test of Success and Failure,	143
XVI.	The Test of Want and Relief,	152
XVII.	The Withered Hand,	163
XVIII.	The Smitten Mouth,	173
XIX.	The Silence of Christ,	181
XX.	Waiting on the Lord,	190
XXI.	The Cleansing Blood,	198
XXII.	Dwelling Among Lions,	207
XXIII.	The Blessings of Time,	215
XXIV.	The Fall of Balaam,	225
XXV.	The Man Nearest to God,	235
XXVI.	Why Weepest Thou?	243
XXVII.	Holy Joy,	252
XXVIII.	Looking Unto Jesus,	263

Heart Talks.

I.

MY CONVERSION.

THE first deep religious impression I can recall occurred in my boyhood. A protracted-meeting was being conducted in the town where I was raised. Several preachers were in attendance, and I, a lad of eight or ten years, was present a few times. At the close of the services, and on the departure of the ministers, I remember to have gone into a room alone, and, casting myself on the bed, wept a considerable while. At that time I felt a great softness of heart, and realized a decided drawing to, and preference for, the Christian life; but in the course of a few weeks it all passed away.

At the age of nineteen or twenty, on returning from college, I joined a fashionable Church of another denomination from that in which I had been raised. This step was brought about mainly through certain social influences, and in connecting myself with that branch of Christ's Church there was no change of heart, nor indeed any proper spiritual impression.

At the age of twenty-six, with a young wife and two children, God found me. For years I had not been to church, avoided preachers, laughed at religion, and was on the broad road to ruin. I regarded not the Sabbath, was a great smoker of tobacco, had got to imbibing wine occasionally, and was very profane. My temper at this time had become ungovernable, and the devil undoubtedly had me.

In the place where the Savior found me there were no churches and no Christians. Instead of this, there was any amount of card-playing, horse-racing, and whisky-drinking. I did not take up with these last three things, but, nevertheless, spiritually I was in a lost condition.

The way my conversion took place has been an unceasing wonder to me, as well as source of endless gratitude.

Let the reader remember that there were no churches in miles of me, and no preachers or Christians around.

The business of the store in which I was employed as clerk and bookkeeper fell off greatly during the summer of 1874. I used to walk up and down the lonely building and meditate. Christ had got me at last to a place where I was quiet, and could think.

The thought which repeatedly arose to my mind, and with ever-increasing bitterness and sorrow, was that I was a failure; that at twenty-six years of age I had done nothing and was nothing.

I can see now that the Spirit was very busy with me; I could not recognize his work so readily then, but it is all clear now. He had no one to use in that part of the country to teach me, and so worked directly upon my mind and heart. Repeatedly, when alone in the store, I have buried my face in the piles of goods on the counter, and wept the saddest of tears. Then there would come longings to redeem my life, and be a true man. But I was profoundly ignorant as to what steps to take.

At this juncture I wrote two or three lines to my mother, saying, "I am determined to be a better man, and when I am a better man, I am going to pray."

The reply of my mother was all the help of a human character I obtained in my conversion. She wrote a hasty and brief answer, in these words:

"MY DEAR SON,—I am delighted to hear of your good resolutions. But you have made a great mistake. Do n't wait to be a better man before you pray, but pray, and you *will* be a better man.
    "Affectionately,   YOUR MOTHER."

This note brought a perfect flood of light to my mind. I saw I had been putting the cart before the horse. Like the lightning illumines the whole landscape with a sudden flash, so God used the simple words of my mother to clear up the uncertainty and darkness, and I saw in an instant, and that most vividly, what I had to do. I must pray, and keep at it until something happened.

That Thursday night I knelt down to pray at my bedside for the first time since my boyhood. My young wife looked perfectly astounded at the act. I do not believe that if a wild animal had leaped through the window into the room, she could have been more amazed than she was at the spectacle of her kneeling husband; but I always possessed a goodly amount of will-power and what is commonly called backbone, and so prayed on. Still I did not believe God would have mercy on such a sinner as myself; and so He did not, for without faith it is impossible to please Him.

Friday night I was on my knees again before retiring; but it seemed to me that God was far away in heaven, and I was down here on earth, and I did not see how He could save me. And so He did not, for here was unbelief again.

On Saturday night I went again through the melancholy and apparently fruitless struggle. I arose with neither light nor comfort, but full of determination to press on and pray on until something happened.

On Sunday the store was closed, and I had the entire Sabbath at home. After breakfast I walked out in a grove near the house, and there, hidden from view, knelt down amid the trees, and with longing eyes looked up through an open space into the blue heaven. I told God that I gave Him myself and all I had, that I wanted salvation and rest, and please to take me. I pleaded with Him in this way for quite a while, and discontinued I know not why. I walked thoughtfully back to the house, and took my seat by the side of a center-table in the room. I picked up the Bible to read, and had scarcely read a line when suddenly I was converted. Such a peace and rest flooded my soul as I had never felt before in my life, and it was so new, so sweet, so strangely blissful, so melting, that I burst into tears, and cried out to my wife on the opposite side of the table, "O Laura, I am not going to hell after all!"

I went across the room, and poured water into the basin to bathe my tear-stained face. But I found that a fountain was flowing which I could not stop; and a blessed, beautiful love and peace was in me that water could not wash away.

In a few hours the ecstasy was gone; but I was a changed man. Moreover, everybody saw it, at home and abroad.

In going from my house to the store, two miles

away, I would pray three times before I got there. I had the places picked out, one in a deep wooded valley, one in a willow thicket in the middle of the field, and one on the top of a hill, protected from view by a clump of trees.

I was very ignorant in regard to spiritual things; but I kept on praying, read much in a Bible which I carried in my pocket; began family prayer, although it came near choking me to pray before my wife and neighbors who dropped in; and, in addition, talked to everybody who would listen to me about this new strange, wonderful life which had come to me.

Two men drove up to the store one day, and after the exchange of salutations, pulled out a flask of whisky and asked me if I would take a drink with them. I replied: "No, I thank you. Now, as you have offered something to me, let me read something to you out of this Book."

I began drawing my little Bible out of my pocket; but the instant they saw what it was, they gave their horse a sharp cut with the whip, and without a word of farewell dashed down the road. To this day I can recall their astonished look, discomfited faces, and rapid retreat.

Yet with this completely changed life, I could not understand many things about my own experience. I could not see why that delightful joy which had filled me that Sabbath morning had left me. I knew it was from God; but why should it depart? It did not abide, although it left me a changed man. The constant query of my mind was relative to that new sweet emotion that swept over me. Was it salvation, or God simply encouraging and drawing me on to salvation yet to come? Let the reader remember I had no one to look to or advise with.

One day there came an unutterable longing to experience again the same sweet spiritual sensation which had flooded me for the first time a few days before. In my rummaging over the library for religious books I had found an old work, wherein I read of a devout woman who was so humble that she always prayed to God on her face. It made a deep impression on me. I was standing on the gallery of the store thinking about it with that hungry heart of mine. Looking up and down the long road, I saw no one in sight, whereupon I stretched myself upon the ground, put my face down in the grass, and asked God to please grant me the same blessed joy He had given me in my house that Sabbath morning, that I might know I was His. Instantly I was filled with holy joy, the identical first experience. I arose from the ground all smiles, and with happy tears flowing down my face. But in a few hours it was all gone again.

So passed ten days or two weeks away, when I became hungry for spiritual instruction. There was so much I did not understand, and craved to know.

I determined to go to a Methodist preacher, and lay the whole case before him. So, saddling my horse, I rode twelve miles to Yazoo City, and called on the Rev. R. D. Norsworthy. There were other preachers in the town; but it is significant that I felt drawn to go to a minister of the Church of my mother, and in which I had been brought up.

This Methodist pastor said afterwards, that as he saw me walking towards his gate he felt, as he looked at my face, that he had business on his hands. Telling him that I desired to speak with him on spiritual matters, he dismissed all from the room, asked me to be seated, and to tell him what was on my mind.

Something of my ignorance of religious phrases and terms can be seen in one of the first utterances that fell from my lips. The preacher must have been amused, if not amazed. I said in a broken voice: "Mr. Norsworthy, I am an awakened man; but I do not think I am convicted yet;" and promptly burying my face in my hands, burst into a flood of tears.

From this occurrence it can be seen that the heart and head do not always run equally together in the race for heaven. It is possible to be all right in soul, and not understand theology. The spiritual part of a divine blessing can come on the lightning express, while the intellectual part may arrive some hours or days later on the freight.

The preacher saw at once that I was a converted man; but determined that God should tell me, and in His own way and time. He, however, quoted a number of Bible passages to me, which brought floods of light then and afterwards.

So, on returning home, when this beautiful joy swept again into my heart, I knew it was the Spirit's witness to my salvation and sonship. I pored over the Bible, devoured every good book I could find, prayed on my knees six or seven times a day, talked religion to everybody, stirred up the whole country, saw my wife and sister both converted in less than a month, and became blessedly established in a few weeks.

II.

CALL TO THE MINISTRY.

SOON after my conversion, I felt drawn to join the Methodist Church. Hiring a buggy, I drove into Yazoo City one Saturday with my wife and two children. The little ones were brought in to be baptized. We all came to the altar together, the whole family being given to God at the same hour. On returning to my pew, I was melted with holy love, and wept convulsively with my head bowed on the bench before me. An old, grayheaded member of the Church, Brother Hunter by name, came over to me, and, giving me his hand, wept also as he tried to speak.

It was while sitting in this pew I felt the first call to preach. As my eyes fell on the preacher who had taken me into the Church, and who was now speaking in the pulpit, a voice whispered within me, "That is your place."

I was astonished, and yet thrilled. In another moment this verse was deeply impressed upon me, and I was less familiar with it than many other passages: "How beautiful upon the mountains are the feet of him that bringeth good tidings, that publisheth peace; that bringeth good tidings of good, that publisheth salvation; that saith unto Zion, Thy God reigneth!"

As these words lingered like a strain of melody in my heart, I found a great desire springing up to do as the verse said. It seemed, however, as I thought upon the matter, among the impossibilities, and so I dismissed the thought, and remembered the impression no more for days.

After this my pastor paid me a short visit, and while walking with him along the road, he suddenly turned, and said, "My brother, you ought to preach."

Again I was both pleased and yet disturbed. Then followed several weeks of a most remarkable struggle in regard to the matter. An impression was on me that I must preach, accompanied with delightful divine touches upon the soul; but as I reasoned against and resisted it, a profound gloom would come upon me for hours.

While in this state of mind I spoke one day to a friend and relative, who was an unconverted man, telling him of the impression upon me, but that I felt so unworthy that it seemed to me if I should enter the pulpit some one ought to kick me out. His reply was, "If you feeel this way, you evidently ought not to preach."

His answer brought no relief, but cast me down

more than ever. It was some time afterward before I got the light to see that he, being an unregenerated man, was in no condition to give advice in spiritual matters. I also got to see that a sense of unworthiness is a good and proper feeling for one to have who enters upon the sacred vocation of the ministry. I saw that while I had expressed myself unfortunately in confessing to my sense of unworthiness, yet back of the faulty words was a right spirit and state of heart with which God was well pleased.

There were two approaches to the house where I lived,—one which skirted a field and went over a hill to the high road, and another much shorter, which passed through a narrow, dark valley of several hundred yards in extent. This valley was so filled with forest trees, growing up its steep sides and bending over at the summit, that even in the daytime the place was shadowy and gloomy-looking; but at night the darkness was intense, and on starlit nights it was exceedingly difficult to see the path which wound about through the trees, crossing and recrossing the little branch of water that tinkled down the center.

One night I entered this place, trying to persuade myself that it was impossible for me to preach, that I did not have the ability, the eloquence, and many other things that I thought to be necessary. I found that as I thus mentally argued against my entering upon such a calling and life, that I was becoming more and more darkened in mind and wretched in soul. About the time I reached the darkest portion of the woods, I felt that the valley was not as black as my spirit in its conscious lack of all spiritual light and comfort. I was in such misery, and there came upon me such a horror of darkness, that I fell upon the ground, and rolled upon the leaves in the most acute and overwhelming distress.

Suddenly, I know not why, I looked up, and cried out, "Lord, I will preach," when instantly the glory of God filled me, the dark valley fairly flashed and glittered, and laughing, crying, and shouting, I leaped along the path, jumped the branch, ran up the hillside, on the top of which was my home, and fairly quivering with joy, and with my face all aglow with the happiness in me, I stood before my wife in the sitting-room, crying out, "I will preach."

This joy remained in me for several days, when I began looking again at my unfitness. I remembered I had never been trained to speak in public, had not gone to a theological college, was far from sure that I could preach a sermon, etc. Whereupon all the old gloom came back upon me.

I struggled along with the depression the best I could while I attended to the work at the store. One day I was out on a collecting tour, and had ridden from house to house, and plantation to plantation, with my bills and accounts, and was that wretched I could scarcely speak to the people I was calling upon. Happening to pass in the neighborhood of my home in the afternoon, my wife, seeing my fatigue and melancholy, insisted on my stopping while she had me a lunch prepared. I sat down at the table mechanically, and did not even notice what was placed before me. I fear I did not hear her when she spoke to me. I was in a gloom that God himself was putting on me to bring me to my senses.

I can not tell why I did so, but without any mental process leading up to the speech, without having anticipated saying it a minute beforehand, and just as if it was hurled out of me by some internal force, I struck the table with my clenched hand, and cried, "I will preach the gospel!" Instantly the glory of God filled me, so that I laughed, wept, and rejoiced uncontrollably for fully a half hour.

Will the reader be out of patience with me, when I state that, in spite of all this evident will of God in my case, I allowed Satan in the next hour to direct my mind to the fact that I was no speaker, never had been one, and that the twenty-sixth year of one's life was a very late hour to get ready for such an important work. The consequence was, another spell of gloom followed. For in less than a minute after I allowed the doubt to enter, God's Spirit withdrew, and left me in the old-time horrible gloom.

It gives me pleasure to state that the next battle I fought proved a victory, and one that was glorious, complete, and permanent.

Several days after the occurrence just related, I was sitting one night in company with my wife in our room. She was sewing by lamplight on one side of the center-table, while I was on the other side unable to read, talk, and scarcely think, because of the burden on the heart and conflict in the mind. Forgetful of her presence and everything else in my misery, suddenly as had happened twice before, without any studied purpose of saying such words, here they came again, "God helping me, I *will* preach the gospel," when such a flash of light, such a tender, melting, thrilling joy entered my soul, that I leaped to my feet, and stood all trembling and transfigured before my wife. To this day I recall her words: "Beverly, how can you doubt God's will in this matter any longer after what he has just done for you?"

Thank God! I never did any more. From that hour to this, there has never been a question in my mind but that God, in his infinite condescension, called me to preach the gospel of his blessed Son, the Lord Jesus Christ.

A few weeks after this, I was recommended by the

Church Conference of Yazoo City, Rev. R. D. Norsworthy pastor, to the Quarterly Conference for license to preach. The last named body licensed and recommended me to the Mississippi Annual Conference. A single vote was cast against me; it was that of the old man who had wept over me when I joined the Church. He doubtless could not see how so much could be done for a young man in so brief a period: converted July 12th, and here in October licensed to preach and recommended to the Annual Conference. It all looked like undue haste and general prematureness to him. He did not know that sometimes people can live a year in one day, and that God can marvellously carry on His work in a surrendered soul and life.

I was outside of the church while they were balloting on my name, having been requested to withdraw. I can see the old brick building now, the place where I had gone to Sunday-school as a child, and attended Church with my mother, brother, and sisters. My mind was not on what the Quarterly Conference was doing inside. I was in the shadow of an old tree which grew near the pavement, and was looking up at the distant stars, filled with thoughts of Christ, and feeling what an honor and responsibility was laid on me in preaching the gospel.

Some one came to the church door and called me.

I went in, and was told by the presiding elder, the Rev. H. H. Montgomery, that I had been licensed to preach, and recommended for the traveling connection in the Mississippi Annual Conference, the next session of which was to be held in December, 1874, in the town of Hazelhurst.

That night, when assigned to a room in the hospitable home of the Methodist pastor, I could not sleep; but lay thinking and praying on the bed. It seemed so strange to be a preacher. Then I felt so keenly my littleness and helplessness that I was quite cast down. Suddenly I had such a view of Christ presenting me to his Father, protecting and covering me by his love, grace, and power, that I was filled with one of the sweetest blessings I had ever experienced.

Having a long ride before me the next day, I arose before daylight without disturbing the family, saddled my horse, and left Yazoo City asleep behind me, while the firmament was twinkling above my head, and the morning star hung, a great orb of beauty, in the east, the beautiful forerunner of the unrisen sun.

I was five miles from town when the day began to break. The cotton and corn fields had little spots and banks of silver haze upon them. A sweetness and freshness was in the air of the early dawn that was like an elixir to brain and heart. The hills were standing up in the indistinct light, solemn and gray, like great altars. A slight mist on their heads looked like rising incense. Nature seemed to be sacrificing to God. I was drinking it all into my already overflowing soul, when fully a quarter of a mile away, on one of the hills, I heard a negro man singing. His voice was rich, deep, and solemn. The hymn was a plaintive old melody. The words and music God brought to me through the misty, tremulous, beautiful morning air were:

How the sacred song echoed and re-echoed over the fields, in the valley, and was thrown back from the opposite hillsides! I was almost breathless, while the words "heavenly race" and "immortal crown" seemed to linger the longest.

The singer was hidden from me in the trees on the hill. He knew not that his song was reaching, filling, and blessing me, and this made it all the more powerful. I had checked the canter of my horse, and was walking him along the road, that I might catch every strain and hear every word. The singer was deliberate. He may have been employed in some kind of work, and hence took his time; so that a full minute elapsed, giving the strains of the first verse full time to die away in the distance before he resumed again. This time it was:

> "A cloud of witnesses around,
> Hold thee in full survey;
> Forget the steps already trod,
> And onward urge thy way."

This time I felt the wonderful strengthening and girding power of the words, and said most fervently, "Lord, it shall be so."

Again, after a pause, came another verse, thrown outward by the mellow, solemn voice of the singer:

> "'T is God's all animating voice
> That calls thee from on high;
> 'T is His own hand presents the prize
> To thine aspiring eye."

O, how the strain and words sank into the soul! The contrast between earth and heaven was so profoundly felt. The littleness of the one, and the greatness and blessedness of the other, seemed to be two facts unquestioned by the glowing heart.

As the Negro sang that morning, would that all could have heard him in one of God's natural temples! And yet, as far as I could see, there was but one listener and worshiper beside himself. What a pity not to have heard such a sacred song, with the sides of the valley for sounding-boards, the opaline sky for a ceiling, the floating mist on the hilltops like incense rising from majestic altars, while the silent woods and fragrant canebrakes seemed actually to be drinking the scene and sound in, like the solitary listener!

The singer reached the fourth stanza. How triumphantly it rang out! Not a note or word was lost:

> "That crown, with peerless glories bright,
> Which shall new luster boast,
> When victors' wreaths and monarch's gems
> Shall blend in common dust."

The world looked very little, and its honors and rewards very contemptible, under the words of the last verse. Heaven seemed the only thing worth living for. The heart was all melted, and the tears dropped fast.

I had reined in my horse to hear the last strain and word of the hymn which God had sent to me. I also wanted to impress the scene upon my mind, and carry it away with me, a precious mental treasure forever. And I did so.

After a little, when the silence reigned unbroken over the fields, and the singer had gone, I touched my horse and galloped swiftly away. I had many miles to go, and much to do that day. I had to tell my employer that God had work for me; I wanted to see my mother and get her blessing; and then I wanted to reach my own home by sundown, where my wife was waiting to hear what had happened, and what I was going to do.

All this was attended to that day with a glad and overflowing heart. The die had been cast. I had crossed my Rubicon. I had turned my back on the old-time life forever, and was now the Lord's. I was His servant and ambassador from this time forth to preach his gospel.

But I took that morning picture with me. To this hour I see the dawning day, the outspread misty fields, the motionless woods, the silent, solemn hills, while floating over it all I hear the plaintive song of the unseen Negro singer, whom God sent forth to nerve, encourage, and bless the soul of a young, newly-made preacher.

May he, with all others in the Christian ministry, be able to join in the last verse of the already quoted song:

> "Blest Savior, introduced by thee,
> Have I my race begun;
> Till, crowned with vict'ry, at thy feet
> I'll lay my honors down."

III.

MY SANCTIFICATION.

I ALWAYS believed in the doctrine in a general way, but not in the way particular. That is, I recognized it as being true in our standards and religious biographies; but was not so quick to see it in the life and experience of persons claiming the blessing. I was too loyal a Methodist to deny what my Church taught me to believe; but there must have been beams and motes that kept me from the enjoyment of a perfect vision of my brother. Perhaps I was prejudiced; or I had confounded ignorance and mental infirmity with sin; or, truer still, I was looking on a "hidden life," as the Bible calls it, and, of course, could not but blunder in my judgments and conclusions, even as I had formerly erred as a sinner in my estimation of the converted man.

I remember once having been thrown in the company of three ministers who were sanctified men, and their frequent "praise the Lords" was an offense to me. I saw nothing to justify such demonstrativeness. The fact entirely escaped me that a heart could be in such a condition that praise and rejoicing would be as natural as breathing; that the cause of joy rested not in anything external, but in some fixed inward state or possession; that, therefore, perpetual praise could not only be possible, but natural, and in fact irrepressible. But at that time all this was hidden from me, except in a theoretic way, or as mistily beheld in distant lives of saints who walked with God on earth fifty or a hundred years ago.

In my early ministry I was never thrown with a sanctified preacher, nor had I ever heard a sermon on entire sanctification. I beheld the promised life from a Pisgah distance, and came back from the view with a fear and feeling that I should never come into that goodly land. So, when I was being ordained at Conference, it was with considerable choking of voice, and with not a few inward misgivings and qualms of conscience, that I replied to the bishop's questions, that I was "going on to perfection," that I "expected to be made perfect in love in this life," and that I "was groaning after it." Perhaps the bishop himself was disturbed at the questions he asked. Perhaps he thought it was strange for a minister of God and father in Israel, whose life was almost concluded, to be asking a young preacher if he expected to obtain what he himself had never succeeded in getting. Stranger still, if he asked the young prophet if he expected to attain what he really felt was unattainable!

One thing I rejoice in being able to say: That although about that time, while surprised and grieved at the conduct of a man claiming the blessing of sanctification, and although doubts disturbed me then and even afterward, yet I thank God that I have never, in my heart or openly, denied an experience or warred against a doctrine that is the cardinal doctrine of the Methodist Church, and concerning which I solemnly declared to the bishop that I was groaning to obtain. God in his mercy has kept me from this inconsistency—this peculiar denial of my Church and my Lord. Let me further add, that in spite of my indistinct views of sanctification all along, yet ever and anon during my life I have encountered religious people in whose faces I traced spiritual marks and lines—a divine handwriting not seen on every Christain countenance. There was an indefinable something about them, a gravity and yet sweetness of manner, a containedness and quietness of spirit, a restfulness and unearthliness, a far-awayness about them, that made me feel and know that they had a life and experience that I had not; that they knew God as I did not, and that a secret of the Lord had been given to them which had not been committed to me. These faces and lives, in the absence of sanctified preachers and sermons on the subject, kept my faith in the doctrine, in a great degree I suppose, from utterly perishing. Then there were convictions of my own heart all along in regard to what a minister's life should be. Only a month before my sanctification, there was impressed upon me suddenly one day such a sense of the holiness and awfulness of the office and work, that my soul fairly sickened under the consciousness of its own shortcomings and failures, and was made to cry out to God. Moreover, visions of an unbroken soul-rest, and a constant abiding spiritual power, again and again came up before the mind as a condition possible and imperative. A remarkable thing about it is, that these impressions came to one who had enjoyed the peace of God daily for fifteen years.

At the Seashore Camp-ground, in 1888, after having preached at eleven o'clock, the writer came forward to the altar as a penitent convicted afresh under his own sermon, that he was not what he should be, nor what God wanted him to be and was able to make him. Many will remember the day and hour, and the outpouring of the Holy Spirit at the time. I see now that my soul was reaching out, even then, not for the hundredth or thousandth blessing (for these I had before obtained), but what is properly called the *Second* Blessing. I was even then convicted by the Holy Ghost in regard to the presence of inbred sin in a justified heart.

Nearly a year afterward I instituted a series of revival services in Carondelet Street Church, with the Rev. W. W. Hopper as my helper. At all the morning meetings the preacher presented the subject of entire sanctification. It was clearly and powerfully held up as being obtained instantaneously through consecration and faith. Before I received the blessing myself, I could not but be struck with the presence and power of the Holy Ghost. While urging the doctrine one morning, the preacher received such a baptism of glory that for minutes he was helpless; and while we were on our knees supplicating for this instantaneous sanctification, the Holy Spirit fell here and there upon individuals in the assembly, and shouts of joy and cries of rapture went up from the kneeling congregation in a way never to be forgotten. The presence of God was felt so overwhelmingly and so remarkably that I could not but reason after this manner: Here is being presented the doctrine of instantaneous sanctification by faith. If it were a false doctrine, would God thus manifest himself? Would the Holy Ghost descend with approving power upon a lie? Does he not invariably withdraw his presence from the preacher and people when false doctrine is presented? But here He is manifesting Himself in a most remarkable manner. The meeting or hour that is devoted to this one subject is the most wonderful meeting and hour of all. The service fairly drips with unction. Shining faces abound. Christ is seen in every countenance. If entire sanctification obtained instantaneously is a false doctrine, is not the Holy Ghost actually misleading the people by granting His presence and favor, and showering His smiles at the time when this error or false doctrine is up for discussion and exposition? But would the Spirit thus deceive? Irresistibly and with growing certainty I was led to see that the truth was being presented from the pulpit, and that the Holy Ghost, who always honors the truth when preached, was falling upon sermon, preacher, and people, because it was the truth. And by the marvelous and frequent display of His presence and power at each and every sanctification meeting He was plainly setting to it the seal of His approval and indorsement, and declaring unmistakably that the doctrine which engrossed us was of heaven, and was true.

One morning a visitor—a man whom I admire and love—made a speech against entire sanctification, taking the ground that there was nothing but a perfect consecration and growth in grace to look for; that there was no second work or blessing to be experienced by the child of God. This was about the spirit and burden of his remarks. At once a chill fell upon the service, that was noticed then and commented on afterward. The visitor was instantly replied to by one who had just received the blessing, and as immediately the presence of God was felt and manifested. And to the proposition made—that all who believed in an instantaneous and entire sanctification would please arise—at once the whole audience, with the exception of five or six individuals, arose simultaneously. It was during this week that the writer commenced seeking the blessing of sanctification. According to direction, he laid everything on the altar—body, soul, reputation, salary, indeed everything. Feeling at the time justified, having peace with God, he could not be said to have laid his sins on the altar; for, being forgiven at that moment, no sin was in sight. But he did this, however: he laid *inbred sin* upon the altar; a something that had troubled him all the days of his converted life—a something that was felt to be a disturbing element in his Christian experience and life. Who will name this something? It is called variously by the appellations of original sin, depravity, remains of sin, roots of bitterness and unbelief, and by Paul it is termed "the old man;" for, in writing to Christians, he exhorts them to put off "the old man," which was corrupt. Very probably there will be a disagreement about the name while there is perfect recognition of the existence of the thing itself. For lack of a title that will please all, I call the dark, disturbing, warring principle "that something." It gives every converted man certain measures of inward disturbance and trouble. Mind you, I do not say that it compels him to sin, for this "something" can be kept in subjection by the regenerated man. But it always brings disturbance, and often leads to sin. It is a something that leads to hasty speeches, quick tempers, feelings of bitterness, doubts, suspicions, harsh judgments, love of praise, and fear of men. At times there is a momentary response to certain temptations that brings, not merely a sense of discomfort, but a tinge and twinge of condemnation. All these may be, and are, in turn, conquered by the regenerated man; but there is battle and wounds; and often after the battle a certain uncomfortable feeling within that it was not a perfect victory. It is a something that at times makes devotion a weariness, the Bible to be hastily read instead of devoured, and prayer a formal approach instead of a burning interview with God that closes with reluctance. It makes Church-going at times not to be a delight, is felt to be a foe to secret and spontaneous giving, causes religious experience to be spasmodic, and presents within the soul a constant, abiding, and unbroken rest. Rest there is; but it is not continuous, unchanging, and permanent. It is a something that makes true and noble men of

God, when appearing in the columns of a Christian newspaper in controversy, to make a strange mistake, and use gall instead of ink, and write with a sword instead of a pen. It is a something that makes religious assemblies sing with great emphasis and feeling:

"*Prone to wander*, Lord, I feel it."

It is an echo that is felt to be left in the heart, in which linger sounds that ought to die away forever. It is a thread or cord-like connection between the soul and the world, although the two have drifted far apart. It is a middle ground, a strange medium, upon which Satan can and does operate, to the inward distress of the child of God, whose heart at the same time is loyal to his Savior, and who feels that if he died even then, he would be saved.

Now that something I wanted out of me. What I desired was not the power of self-restraint (that I had already), but a spirit naturally and unconsciously meek. Not so much a power to keep from all sin, but a *deadness* to sin. I wanted to be able to turn upon sin and the world the eye and ear and heart of a dead man. I wanted perfect love to God and man, and a perfect rest in my soul all the time. This dark "something" that prevented this life, I laid on the altar, and asked God to consume it as by fire. I never asked God once at this time for pardon. That I had in my soul already. But it was cleansing, sin eradication, I craved. My prayer was for sanctification.

After the battle of consecration came the battle of faith. Both precede the perfect victory of sanctification. Vain is consecration without faith to secure the blessing. Hence men can be consecrated, and not know the blessing of sanctification. I must believe there is such a work in order to realize the grace. Here were the words of the Lord that proved a foundation for my faith: "Every devoted thing is most holy unto the Lord." "The blood of Jesus Christ, his Son, cleanseth us from *all* sin." Still again: "The altar sanctifieth the gift." In this last quotation is a statement of a great fact. The altar is greater than the gift; and whatsoever is laid upon the altar becomes sanctified or holy. It is the altar that does the work. The question arises: Who and what is the altar? In Hebrews xiii, 10-12, we are told. Dr. Clarke, in commenting upon the passage, says the altar here mentioned is Jesus Christ. All who have studied attentively the life of our Lord can not but be impressed with the fact that in his wondrous person is seen embraced the priest, the lamb, and the altar. He did the whole thing; there was no one to help. As the victim He died, as the priest He offered Himself, and His divine nature was the altar upon which the sacrifice was made. The Savior, then, is the Christian's altar. Upon Him I lay myself. The altar sanctifies the gift. The blood cleanses from all sin, personal and inbred. Can I believe that? Will I believe it? My unbelief is certain to shut me out of the blessing; my belief as certainly shuts me in. The instant we add a perfect faith to a perfect consecration, the work is done and the blessing descends. As Paul says, "We which have believed do enter into rest."

All this happened to the writer. For nearly three days he lived in a constant state of faith and prayer. He believed God; he believed the work was done before the witness was given.

On the morning of the third day—may God help me to tell it as it occurred!—the witness was given. In was about nine o'clock in the morning. That morning had been spent from daylight in meditation and prayer. I was alone in my room in the spirit of prayer, in profound peace and love, and in the full expectancy of faith, when suddenly I felt that the blessing was coming. By some delicate instinct or intuition of soul I recognized the approach and descent of the Holy Ghost. My faith arose to meet the blessing. In another minute I was literally prostrated by the power of God. I called out again and again: "O my God! my God! and glory to God!" while billows of fire and glory rolled in upon my soul with steady, increasing force. The experience was one of fire. I recognized it all the while as the baptism of fire. I felt that I was being consumed. For several minutes I thought I would certainly die. I knew it was sanctification. I knew it as though the name was written across the face of the blessing and upon every wave of glory that rolled in upon my soul.

Can not God witness to purity of heart as he does to pardon of sin? Are not his blessings self-interpreting? He that impresses a man to preach, that moves him unerringly to the selection of texts and subjects, that testifies to a man that he is converted, can he not let a man know when he is sanctified? In answer, read Hebrews x, 14: "For by one offering He hath forever perfected them that are sanctified, whereof the Holy Ghost also is a witness to us."

I knew I was sanctified, just as I knew fifteen years before that I was converted. I knew it, not only because of the work itself in my soul, but through the Worker. He, the Holy Ghost, bore witness clearly, unmistakably, and powerfully to his own work; and although years have passed away since that blessed morning, yet the witness of the Holy Spirit to the work is as clear to-day as it was then.

IV.

CALL TO THE EVANGELISTIC WORK.

SOME good people have expressed great skepticism in regard to a special call from God to evangelize. They can understand a regular call to the ministry, but fail to see and believe in an impression from the Holy Ghost for that particular work.

There are several facts which should cause them to give perfect credence to the statements of preachers who have been thus impressed, anointed, and separated for the calling and peculiar labor.

One fact is the existence of such a spiritual office in the kingdom of Christ. Among the Savior's gifts to the Church, in addition to prophets, apostles, pastors, and teachers, Paul mentions the evangelist. The Scripture does not leave us in doubt as to who and what he is; and so, after telling us in Ephesians how he is to "perfect the saints" and "edify the body of Christ," etc., we are shown in another book a vivid, life-size picture of one at work. The portrait is that of Philip, sent here and there, caught away to this place, having a revival in another place, and always filled with the power of the Holy Ghost. The Bible says about him, that he was an evangelist; the

Scriptural idea of such an office being that of a man constantly on the move for God, and preaching as he goes. Certainly the conclusion is clear, that if there be such a spiritual office and work, there will be a call to that effect from the Holy Ghost.

Our bishops ought not to be surprised at such a call when, being preachers already, they state that they were moved by the Holy Spirit to take upon them the office and work of a bishop in the Church of God; a work and office decidedly different in many respects from that of a pastor. From comparative obscurity he springs into prominence; from a small salary he is advanced to a large one; from a small local influence to lifetime power; from being ruled to ruling others. This is a great change; yet they say, before a large crowd of listening preachers and laymen, that they have been moved by the Holy Ghost to take upon them this office.

It certainly appears to the writer that when an evangelist arises, and says that, as a preacher, the call of God has come to him to enter upon a work which means increased labor, uncertain income, and oftentimes lifetime reproach, our bishops ought to be the last to doubt him. If the two calls of bishop and evangelist are brought under the searching light of the Gospel, which seems to be the most spiritual and heavenly, and which life looks most like that of the Man of Nazareth and Galilee?

Again, our missionaries ought not to be surprised. They were preachers, and yet upon them, as such, came the call to cross the sea and labor with the heathen. Not every minister of the gospel has this call. In addition they feel impressed to go to certain countries. One man is convinced he must labor in Africa, another in Japan, a third in China, a fourth in Alaska, and so on through the list. He who calls them to be missionaries knows their mental and physical fitness for certain parts of the world, and whispers India, Egypt, or some island of the sea.

Is it not strange that the Church, with these facts about the bishops and missionaries before them, should wonder at the special call of God to some of his servants to evangelize.

There are other facts which, if mentioned, would be seen to make an unanswerable argument for the necessity of the work of a true evangelist in the Church. But the scope and design of this chapter will not allow me to bring them forward. Some of them the reader will not have much difficulty in guessing. They all confirm the fact of a distinct divine call to the evangelistic work. It may be a call for life, or for a shorter period. Nevertheless it comes, has come, and will continue to come to certain ones of the servants of God. It came to me. It may be removed, but as yet is upon me. Moreover, I did not want to be an evangelist. When it was first suggested to me by a friend in the beginning of the year 1891, the thought filled me with great pain. I was perfectly satisfied with my work as a pastor. Have always been happy in it, and successful as well. Wedded as I was to the life, to the duties as well as pleasures of the pastorate, the reader can see it would take a good deal to get me out of it.

The first voice in this direction was an impression which came vividly to me one day, that I would yet be one. This was in the early part of 1893.

A second time, weeks afterward, it came upon me while looking on my congregation at First Church, which body of people I most deeply loved. The impression was as clear to the mind as print to the eye, "You must leave them and go out for Me."

A third time it came, while I was on my face in the altar of my church, surrounded by a line of penitents and seekers after pardon and holiness. The whisper came to me, "You must be an evangelist." As the word evangelist was impressed upon my mind this time, a most heavenly sweetness filled my soul, and a peace so deep and exquisite came upon me, that I felt my heart would fairly melt within me. I wept

CALL TO THE EVANGELISTIC WORK. 41

silently on my face before the Lord, and whispered back, "I will go, Lord."

At this time God was pleased to send me a double confirmation of the call. One was in the general conviction of the people that I ought to be and would be an evangelist. This corresponds with what takes place when a man is called to preach the gospel; others are impressed at the same time that he should do so.

The other confirmation consisted in numerous "calls" from every direction for evangelistic help in meetings. The doors already began to open.

One day, under an unusually deep impression that I must enter upon such a life, I spoke out suddenly to a member of my family, and said, "I believe God is going to swing me from Massachusetts to California."

How well this has been fulfilled is well-known to thousands of people in the land.

After this, on a certain occasion when I had permitted myself to look at the toil, hardship, and uncertain support of the calling, the long absences from home it would entail, and other disagreeable features that can readily be conjectured, God visited me in another way. The mind of the Spirit was made known to me in a very different and painful manner. An impression vivid as lightning was shot through me, that was as quickly comprehended as though it had been language. It was to this effect: "If you do not go, I will lock up the Bible to you."

I can never forget the shocked and distressed feeling of that moment. I was perfectly conscious that God was speaking to me through his Spirit, and that if I did not yield and go, the peculiar judgment mentioned above would be visited upon me, and I, who had been unfolding the Bible and preaching four times a week with most delightful ease to my people, would find the sacred volume in my hands locked and sealed.

Still later than this, while in the church one day during service, I had an open-eyed, waking vision of a broad landscape filled with church spires, and from whose belfries came the sound of ringing bells. I saw men standing before these buildings, looking toward and beckoning to me. The very bells seemed to call me. My soul was both melted and aroused at the sight, and I do not remember to have doubted or resisted the evangelistic call again.

I made my preparations to leave the pastorate, writing to the bishop of our Conference concerning my intention, and telling him that while I greatly regretted to locate, yet as I was not sick or disabled, I did not see how I could conscientiously ask for a supernumerary relation, and in order to do the right and honest thing I would request a location.

CALL TO THE EVANGELISTIC WORK. 43

This step is a grave one to a Methodist preacher. It meant with me the severing of relations that had been tender and beautiful for eighteen years. It meant the cutting off from my family, in case of my breaking down or death, a certain annual income paid by the Conference to certain claimants. Eighteen laborious years spent in the itinerancy had given me a good right and title to such a fund; but I cut myself and family off from this financial help, as by a single stroke, through my location.

The day I stood up at Conference to ask that I might be located, my heart melted, my voice nearly broke down, and eyes overflowed with the genuine sorrow which I felt. I told the Conference in my farewell remarks, that "I loved the Methodist Church, her doctrines, experiences, bishops, preachers, and people; that I always expected to entertain this love; that a Methodist preacher had baptized me, another had taken me into the Church, a third had married me; that Methodist preachers had baptized and buried my wife and children, and, please God, they should bury me."

The scene will be recalled by many as a tearful time. Some one started a hymn, a number of the brethren came forward and threw their arms around me, and tears were flowing fast all around, when the gavel of the bishop fell with a sharp rap, and I, at my own request, was located in order to become an evangelist.

I know that it was, and is still, a grave step. As an evangelist I have no bishop or presiding elder to look after my family in my absence, or in case of distress and want. In the event of my own personal sickness or exhaustion from the work, I have no salary to live on like a pastor until I get well. I have no Board of Stewards to provide for me, or send me away to some distant place to recuperate and recover, while at the same time the family in my absence is looked after and provided for as though its head were present, engaged in faithful pulpit and pastoral work. All this is lost in becoming an evangelist. Moreover, I knew it when I located.

What a step it was! It helped me to understand better than ever before the Scriptural account of Peter leaping out on the waves to walk to Jesus, and of Abraham going forth at the command of God into strange countries, not knowing whither he went. Here I was with a large family, with heavy monthly expenses to meet, with no bank account, and no Official Board back of me, and yet called to swing out over the land to teach and defend a lost, forgotten, and despised doctrine and experience, with countless battles to fight, ecclesiastical opposition in high places

CALL TO THE EVANGELISTIC WORK. 45

to meet, and the evil forces of two worlds against me. I was to leap out on the waves, and go out at the command of the Lord, not knowing whither I went.

So my new appointment was the United States Circuit. The Savior was my Bishop, the Archangel Gabriel my Presiding Elder; and the angels, ravens, and widow women through the land were my Board of Stewards.

I am still living, traveling, preaching, and rejoicing, while God continues to answer by fire; and wherever I go sinners are saved, backsliders reclaimed, and believers are wholly sanctified to God.

For almost six years I have been preaching a free and full salvation all over our broad land; the first to the sinner, the second to the believer. I have held meetings in nearly every State in the Union, beside the Dominion of Canada. I have witnessed in that time fully fifteen thousand souls converted, reclaimed, and sanctified. My absences from home range from two to seven months at a time. Tight places and trying hours have been many. The body has often been almost exhausted, and the heart at times lonely in a human sense. But the constant smile and presence of Christ has cheered, His hand and voice has called me on to new fields, and as I have joyfully sprung forward to do His will and proclaim a full gospel, He has, without a single exception, on thousands of battle-fields stood by me, and given me the victory.

What matter if devils rage, and human opposition be felt. As I preach the Spirit answers to the Blood, the fire falls upon the Word, sinnners are saved, Christians are sanctified, Christ is uplifted and glorified, and my own soul is thrilled, and blessed, and satisfied. Hallelujah!

V.

REVIVALS.

SOME people have regarded a protracted meeting and a revival as synonymous. But they are far from being the same. The one is a means, and the other should be the end in view. The protracted meeting is inaugurated in order to obtain a revival. But many times the protracted services conclude as they began, without a sign of a genuine, scriptural, Holy Ghost revival.

There are preachers who were once famous for their success in this regard, but who in later life seem to have lost all their former power. There are Churches which were once noted as centers of salvation, that afterward entered upon a period of decline and spiritual lifelessness, reminding one of the Bible description, "Thrice dead and plucked up by the roots." The change in individuals and churches in this regard is painfully evident to all spiritual observers.

A revival on the divine side is the undoubted manifestation of the presence of God, the outpouring of the Holy Ghost and actual conscious arrival of Christ in the midst of the congregation. On the human side it is seen in the conversion of sinners, reclamation of backsliders, sanctification of believers, great joyfulness and activity upon the part of the Church, and deep and solemn conviction in the entire community.

This state of things is brought about by the faithful preaching of the Word and the humble, prayerful waiting upon God of the people. If the protracted meeting lacks these features, the pulpit being without unction, and the pew failing in humility, obedience, supplication, and persistent seeking after God, the services end in utter failure. There is no descent of the Spirit, no quickening of dead hearts, no gladness and freedom, no rout and defeat of sin, no salvation, no anything that is desirable and blessed in the spiritual life.

A genuine revival is unmistakable. It is not only seen, but felt. There was no need to post bills and placards on the walls and fences, stating that the Holy Ghost had fallen upon the disciples in the Upper Room. Some kind of indescribable telegraphy flashed the news everywhere. It is a wireless telegraphy, but none the less certain. As soon as Samaria receives the Word of God, it seems to be known in Jerusalem. When any Church receives the Holy Ghost, it would be easier to hide a city on a hill with its twinkling lights than this fact.

In one of Dr. Finney's revivals, a man was coming in from the country to the town where the work of grace was going on, and when he was still a mile away suddenly felt such a spiritual atmosphere that he was completely melted, and came into the place all hushed and subdued. God had drawn a line of holy grace and power all around the town, and it came to pass that when a man passed it, he was shot through with a dart.

A revival brings with it such a spirit of song, praise, and gladness, such responsiveness in worship, such warmth and power in prayer, such a tender glow through all the service, such waves of joy and glory, that it can not be mistaken. There is no straggling to the meeting. People come in a hurry, and early, and stay late.

In one of my meetings in a Western State, the congregation packed the house one hour before the time of regular evening service, which was 7.30. We were compelled to move the hour of worship up to 6.30. The crowd then filled the building at six o'clock. It was amusing to see the sexton ringing the first and second bell, when the audience had already crowded the house. The writer asked him with a smile why he rang the bell when the congregation had jammed the building before the first belfry summons; was it to let the public know that there was no more room in the house? He failed to understand the little piece of harmless satire, and rang on just the same for five minutes at a time, in obedience, we suppose, to the law of habit, while the people smiled all around at the needless wasted energy of an ecclesiastical machine or automaton.

The revival can come gradually, as the light creeps up over the hills in the east, or suddenly, like a cloudburst. In the first instance there is seen a growing seriousness on the part of the people, a quiet, general melting, and almost before one knows it, the gospel tide is in, and the Church beach is covered with the warm, sunlit waves of salvation. In the second instance, there has been faithful preaching for days, a steady holding on to God by faith and prayer, when on the fourth, fifth, eighth, tenth, or thirteenth day, as the place was more or less difficult, there is a sudden falling of the Spirit upon the people, followed instantly by a melting down, breaking up, and rejoicing time that would defy all description.

These sudden downfalls of the Holy Ghost would read in print as follows: "The revival broke out at eleven or twelve o'clock on such a morning, or eight or nine o'clock on a certain evening;" the point being that all knew when the "Power came down," the Holy Ghost fell on the audience, or the revival really began.

These instantaneous downpourings of the Holy

Spirit have established a remarkable similarity in my mind to certain natural phenomena. As I have witnessed oftentimes in my meetings the hours of prayerful, anxious expectancy of the divine arrival, followed in a single second with the sudden overpowering descent of the Holy Ghost, and that succeeded by a steady outpouring on human hearts and lives, of streams and floods of grace and glory, I have been invariably made to think of a sudden flash of lightning, the sharp, cracklike report of a peal of thunder, and then the steady downpour of a tremendous rain.

I remember it is the same God who does both, and so the likeness should not be so astonishing after all. These are the revivals the writer prefers to see. It is a kind of Noah's Deluge that sweeps skeptics off their feet, chokes their utterances, drives sinners and backsliders to the trees and hills, while the Ark of Salvation, with a full passenger list and cargo, sweeps victoriously over everything, and that in full view of everybody.

No one needs to be told that a revival is going on. Everybody knows it! Its gladsome and yet solemn presence is being felt everywhere in the community. God has granted the writer the privilege of witnessing many of this order, and he has an impression that he is destined to see many more before his work is ended.

On a certain morning in a Southern city, we were

standing facing an audience that had been faithfully preached to for four or five days. God had been, and was working still in hearts, but there was no unusual manifestation of his presence. A hitch or clog was felt to be somewhere. What was it, and where was it?

Suddenly a young lady arose, and confessed to anger, estrangement, and separation from her mother, both parties being members of the Church. With tears dripping down her cheeks, she begged her forgiveness, as she sat on the opposite side of the building. They met midway in the church and were locked in each other's arms, while handkerchiefs were busy in the congregation, though scarcely a sound was to be heard except the low sobs of the mother and daughter referred to above.

In the midst of the quiet, subdued feeling, a gentleman walked down the aisle, and, stopping before a fellow-member of the Church, requested his pardon for some act of the past. In an instant the two men were in each other's arms. Two ladies next arose in different parts of the house, and asked the pastor to forgive them for having talked about him. Both burst into tears as they made the request, and he, with full eyes himself, went to them and gave them his hand with a fervent "God bless you." Next followed two humble confessions from two of the brethren, and two most touching reconciliations, when suddenly, like a flash of lightning, the Holy Ghost fell upon the audience, and there followed a scene I shall never be able to forget, of men and women prostrated under the power of God, some helpless on the floor, some weeping convulsively with faces buried in their hands, some on their feet, laughing, shouting, and clapping their hands, and every soul melted, fired, or filled with the Spirit of God.

We recall a second meeting, where we had reached the fifth day without any notable break. There had been a few souls brought into the light; but the "power" had not come down. One morning, while preaching, the fire fell, the wine of Pentecost arrived, and the congregation looked like drunken people. A man leaped to his feet, crying out in tones that thrilled every heart, "Jesus has come! Jesus has come!" The aisles were filled with laughing, weeping, shouting Christians, a number of them walking or running up and down, clapping their hands and praising God. Sinners were struck down on all sides as if by invisible bolts. Under a single word or touch of the hand of the Spirit-filled Christians, the men slipped from their seats on the floor, or fell down wherever they were. God's people were busy all over the house, talking to and praying with the penitents and seekers; while the shouts of the saved, the cries and wails for mercy, and the hallelujahs of the workers made a combination of sounds astonishing to that town, fearful to hell and its hosts, and all beautiful and delightful to angels and the redeemed of heaven. About twenty-five souls were converted and sanctified at this single service.

A third remarkable revival broke out on the thirteenth day of a meeting I was holding in a city in California. There had been a number of souls saved and sanctified; but what I called the "break" had not come. One Sunday afternoon I was preaching in Peniel Hall to an audience that packed both floor and galleries. The subject was the Baptism of the Holy Ghost, received after the birth of the Spirit, a second work of grace. I was concluding the sermon, while a deep, sweet realization of the presence of God was on my heart and that of others, when suddenly that indescribable flash! crack! and heavenly downpour took place. In other words, the Holy Ghost fell upon scores, if not hundreds, at the same moment. Many will remember the amazing scene. We do not question that a couple of hundred people were all shouting and praising God at the same time. We saw fully fifty people in the gallery standing on their feet, waving their hands and crying, "Glory! Glory to God!" Down on the lower floor the scene was even more wonderful. Numbers rushed to the altar without bidding, a man fell flat on his face in the main aisle, a woman leaped on the platform and began exhorting, while in the midst of shining faces, clapping hands, liberated tongues, singing, shouting, mingled with wails for mercy and cries of victory—salvation free and full flowed like a torrent.

> "O Lord, send the power just now,
> O Lord, send the power just now,
> O Lord, send the power just now,
> And baptize every one."

VI.

ALTAR WORK.

AFTER the sermon should be given the call for penitents and seekers to come to the altar. Not to do this is like throwing a seine in the river, and neglecting to pull it in. It is like firing cannon on the battle-field, with no after-charge, hand-to-hand engagement, and captures. The pulpit is the battery, while the altar is the storm-center of the battle, the place where the greatest struggles are made and the most marvelous victories won. Here Satan and his dark hosts swoop down to fight the working, praying bands of Christ, to darken the minds and sadden the hearts of the seekers, and to resist the heavenly forces, which, while invisible to mortal eyes, are not the less present. Here Doubt, Despondency, and Despair flap their black wings above the altar battle-field, hover over the prostrate and kneeling forms, and settle like vultures to feed on every soul which has been struck down by the devil. Here struggle angels of light with demons of darkness. Here the Holy Ghost descends like a dove, bringing his light, flashing his joy, imparting his life, and at the same time driving back the powers of the infernal world.

Here labor God's devoted followers, reasoning, advising, comforting, cheering, persuading, stimulating, and, in a word, doing everything to help and deliver souls that are endeavoring to find pardon or purity, regeneration or sanctification.

It would not be possible to overestimate the value of these altar services, that are spiritual battle-grounds where sin is slain and the devil defeated; they are plains of glory, where dead lives are quickened, souls born unto God, and men and women baptized with the Holy Ghost and with fire. It not only means a present triumph, but a number of other victories growing out of it and to follow in the lives and labors of those who were restored, renewed, saved, and sanctified at the time. When the "break," as it is called, takes place at the altar, it means that the revival has arrived, and has come to stay. This "break," or sudden fall or outpouring of the Spirit, does not occur in the beginning of the meeting, but generally about the fourth or fifth day. In some instances not before the tenth or fifteenth. It comes as it did at Pentecost, after days of patient, faithful, humble, importunate waiting on God. The formal and fashionable bowing down for a few minutes at the altar, attended by the regulation number of prayers, will never be rewarded with the glories of opening heavens, the descending Dove, the voice of God, and flames of holy fire **falling** upon the soul. It is the protracted upward gaze, the lingering, the continuous asking, which brings down the Holy Ghost.

It is reserved for those who wait and labor to see the most wonderful displays of divine power. They continue to humble themselves, to supplicate, wait, and expect; a half-hour passes away, then an hour; the weak in faith and easily discouraged retire from the church or tabernacle to house or tent. Those who understand the altar and its possibilities, its amazing fulcrum power, its position directly under the Throne of Grace, still linger. Suddenly, like the swift lightning-flash and sharp crack of thunder is followed by a downpour of rain, so suddenly and amazingly the Spirit falls, and showers of heavenly grace come with mighty outpour upon the people. Those who have retired to their beds hear the shouts, outcries, weeping, and laughter, blended with singing and prophesying. Some come running back to look and marvel at the scene of shining faces, clapping hands, and leaping forms. Only those who have patiently waited for the spiritual flash, report, and downpour, best understand and appreciate such a scene of grace.

It requires a good deal to be a successful altar worker. It takes courage to begin the work, and deadness to human opinion to carry it on. It demands patience, wisdom, gentleness, mental quickness, abundance of resource, victorious faith, and power with God to run the altar successfully. John S. Inskip was an acknowledged king here. He could take charge at a moment, when, under a lifeless sermon and drooping service, all hope of victory would be gone from the most sanguine, and lo! in five minutes a great triumph would be seen, and salvation free and full would flow like a mighty tide.

Not all are as gifted and as wonderfully qualified for leadership as Inskip; but all can be effective, and, under God's blessing, have victory over Satan, sin, and the world in every altar battle.

While the writer has seen the wisdom of certain methods, the power attending some kinds of propositions, yet he would not rely on them. He has observed that the indispensable preparation and qualification for a successful altar-worker is a calm, strong faith, and an overflowing experience of holiness. A man full of the Holy Ghost carries with him a sphere of spiritual influence which is soon felt at the altar. His ringing words, shining face, buoyant spirit, perfect confidence in and reliance upon God, inspires faith, causes the seeker to pray and expect and finally to receive with rapturous heart and speech the blessings of pardon and purity.

Yet even the spiritual and successful worker will find, that what will do one time will not answer at another. The Spirit is a free Spirit, and will not work in one groove. He is the leader himself, and would have us to follow him.

Then, again, the mental and spiritual condition of those at the altar is not always the same. Sometimes consecration is to be emphasized; at other times faith. Sometimes prayer is needed; on other occasions the seekers need to be urged to step out on the promises. On some occasions singing is felt to be the need; and again the best work is done when everything is still, and souls are left with Christ, to deal with him personally and alone. In most of my meetings I gladly use all the workers I can get, and have seen God's blessing many times on their labors; but in one of my services I called off the workers, and told the seekers to look to Christ alone, without human help. They did so, and the power began at once to come down, and the fire to fall, and there ensued one of the most wonderful scenes of grace I ever beheld.

Singing is almost invariably used in getting people to the altar; and yet one night, although a volume of inspiring song filled the house, so few were coming forward, that I requested perfect silence, and in the stillness which followed asked all who wanted pardon or holiness to come to the altar, and instantly there was a rush. We never know at first which method the Spirit is going to bless, and so have to follow on softly, looking to him for guidance. He will always lead if we are true to him.

This very difference in his leadings makes us to realize our dependence upon him all the time, and, while using the means of grace and "methods," as we call them, we feel that all are in vain without the Holy Ghost.

As we have just said, we can never tell at first what the Spirit is going to bless. Some days every proper, strong, and wise effort will have been put forth, and there has been no answering fire from heaven, when suddenly, on the utterance of a few simple words, the Holy Ghost will fall.

One day I had done everything I could. The altar was full, and not a soul was "getting through," as it is called. Wearied in mind and body, I arose, and said:

"It is just the question whether we will believe God or not. He has said certain things, and left them in his book. Are they true or not? He says, 'The altar sanctifieth the gift.' Will you believe it or not?"

I had hardly gotten the words out of my mouth, when three or four people leaped to their feet, with illuminated faces and rejoicing in the blessing.

It seemed to me that I had said the same thing repeatedly and much more strikingly before; but somehow the Power came down this time, and the glory of God filled the altar and the people.

In a meeting one night in Kentucky, the altar was filled with men and women; but not a soul could be converted or sanctified. The preacher exhorted and instructed, the brethren prayed, the choir and audience sung, but everything was locked up. Suddenly a young married woman from the country, dressed plainly in calico with an unadorned straw hat on her head, and her baby on her arm, began walking down the side of the altar. As she walked, she with her disengaged hand would touch the bowed heads, or gently pat the shoulders of the seekers. As she did so, she was singing in a sweet, unaffected way:

> "Come, O come to me, said Jesus;
>   Come, and I will give you rest;
> I will take away the burden
>   From thy heavy laden breast;
> No matter who the wand'rer,
>   Nor how far he's gone astray,
> Behold whosoever cometh,
>   I will comfort him to-day."

The scene which followed could scarcely be credited, if it had not been witnessed by hundreds. There was something in the very touch and helplessness of this simple, devout woman, which the Holy Ghost wanted; and as her voice sounded and hand descended, the Spirit fell first upon one and then another, until, leaping to their feet, the altar was surrounded by a now laughing, crying, shouting company of saved and sanctified souls.

As an illustration of good sense and readiness to change and adapt one's self to the hour, with the view of extricating and delivering a meeting that was at a low ebb, I recall the following scene:

The preacher had labored hard in the pulpit for an hour one warm night. The sermon was a failure. Not only the preacher saw it, but the congregation felt it. The preacher sat down and called on a certain minister to conclude. As the latter arose, a number wondered what on earth he proposed doing, and could do. Every eye was on him as he came slowly forward, and stood quietly looking at the great audience before him. He was a young man, and had a task before him which older heads might well have dreaded. For a full minute he stood silent, with a solemn, almost abstracted look, and then began singing:

> "Oh, 't was love, 't was wondrous love,
> The love of God to me;
> It brought my Savior from above,
> To die on Calvary."

At once the vision of the dying Savior was brought up to the minds of the people, and that with an immediate melting effect. Here was no call to come to the altar, no covering up with apologies for a pulpit failure; but an appeal to consider the love of God in the form of his dying Son hanging on the cross. How trifling seemed all excuses for holding back from duty and God with that crucified figure before us!

The hymn, so well known, went on, and when the singer reached the last stanza, the weeping was general, and heads bowed all over the building. The preacher then lifted his hand, and said, "All who would like to come and bow down at the altar for pardon and sanctification, can do so"—and instantly there was a rush from all sides. The people literally fell down, while such soul-sobs and cries went upward as must have made heaven rejoice.

But still a greater than the sudden rescuer of a meeting is the man who understands the "hanging on" principle and spirit.

All who have been much at protracted and camp meetings, have noticed that some preachers or workers would not give up the struggle at the altar, although ten, eleven, and even twelve o'clock at night had come and gone. You left him in the midst of the silent, gloomy line of penitents and seekers. He could not or would not go. He was weary, but still remained with prayer, exhortation, instruction, and song. You remember him leaning against a post near the hour of midnight, singing, "Here I give my all to Thee," and punctuating the hymn with cries, "Have you done it?" "Are you sure all is on the altar?" "Will you put all on now?" "Is everything there?"

Then would follow again the stanza beginning, "Here I give my all to Thee." You grew wearied, and withdrew. In the distance you looked back, and there he was still laboring, a fatigued, overworked man, but unwilling to give up until victory came. He knew God was near, and Christ was faithful. He had a faith worthy of the name. You had not been gone ten minutes when the fire fell, the Spirit answered to the blood, and salvation rolled. Over twenty-five souls were converted and sanctified that night!

Some of my meetings have been remarkable for the weeping spirit of the people. Many nights I have beheld the altar wet, and one time drip with the tears rained upon it. Men may say what they will against the mourner's-bench, but I have found it an unspeakable power for good everywhere I go, and I expect to hold fast to it as a heaven-blessed method of getting people saved and sanctified. I find it becomes a wall between the man and his old life; it is a cross for the old self-life to die upon, and a battle-ground where conflicts between three worlds rage, and where destinies of immortal souls are decided. O, the many, many, many hours I have spent at the altar after the sermon, pressing the battle! No battle can compare for a moment with the importance and results of one of these altar fights. It is a fight, indeed. Angels from above and devils from beneath struggle for the possession of the souls at the altar. Christ is present, the Holy Spirit is there, and Satan is on hand. Oftentimes there are few workers to help the preacher, while a cold, stiff Church membership sit back and look on with skeptical remark or expressionless faces. Great is the temptation of the evangelist to give up at such times; but he who holds on will invariably see victory. Sometimes it comes in a half-hour; sometimes it requires an hour, or two hours, before the rock cracks, the dark, oppressive presence is lifted, and the power and the glory of God come down. Very many are the victories I have seen at the altar, in the joy of which I would forget the anguish of the long waiting and exhausting labor about the wonderful altar rail. Preaching a sermon is easy work compared to this kind of service.

I have been often amused at preachers rushing at the beginning of one of these great altar conflicts to the choir, and there singing most lustily. They wanted to be the brass band on a neighboring hill and furnish music, while from afar they watched the battle. More than once I have told them that they were in easy position—that it is far easier to sing in the choir than work in the altar. It takes but little knowledge of musical notes to bring one into a singing band; but to work patiently and successfully with people at the altar requires a number of things, not only knowledge of God, and a close walk with God, but knowledge of self and knowledge of men. Souls have to be dealt with in wisdom and love. They can not be forced, but must be led. I have seen people driven from the altar by coarse manners and offensive questions. If ever we need good sense, tact, patience, sympathy, love, firmness, and a good religious experience, it is in the altar work. I have not even mentioned the physical exhaustion connected with the work. But at last, when the victory comes; when the faithful instruction and song and prayers have been blessed of God and done their work; when suddenly the light flashes downward from the skies, rapture is poured into penitential souls, devils are cast out, spirits are made free, and songs, shouts, and praises abound; when joyful weeping, happy laughter, handshaking, embracing, and prophesying in the Bible way is the order of the day, then it is seen that it pays to push the fight, press the altar work, and put God to the test.

A single moment of one of these great altar victories recompenses us, in its sweetness and glory, for all the toils of hours and days that have preceded the slow-coming triumph. The pain of long travail is utterly forgotten in the joy that God's truth has been born again into the world in the shape of saved, reclaimed, and sanctified sons and daughters. Praise God for the altar!

VII.

THE SECRET OF THE LORD.

FOR fourteen years of my Christian life I failed to see what was in the Bible expression, "The secret of the Lord." That there was a secret the Scripture taught plainly and repeatedly. The veil in the Tabernacle and Temple, as it hid a certain part of the sanctuary from all eyes but one, and that person a type of Christ, confirmed the fact. Even in the Holy of Holies the two angels bent over the ark as if in investigation and profound study, and so kept prominent the same truth. Later still, Paul speaks of "the mystery of the gospel hid for ages, but revealed in the last days to the saints." And still later, John writes about a white stone given to the Overcomer in the Church, and in it a new name written which no man knoweth saving he that receiveth it.

For quite a while we supposed this mystery and secret was God's unseen, unrecognized presence in the world. After that we thought it meant Christ's incarnation.

We were driven from these and a number of other false conclusions by the explicit statement of God's Word, which at first we did not notice, that the white stone was given not to a repenting sinner, but to an overcomer in the Church. Still farther, that the mystery of the gospel, hid for ages, was revealed in the last days to the saints. If it had been pardon spoken of, and the saving knowledge of God, it would have been a revelation to sinners, and not saints. Then we remembered that pardon had been known from the days of righteous Abel to the present hour; but this peculiar revelation of grace made to saints was given in the "last days."

After this we noticed that Paul declared plainly what the mystery or secret was: "Christ formed within us the hope of glory." Not Christ for us, or with us, but in us. Christ not appearing to a sinner; but Christ entering and dwelling in the Christian. The Divine Visitor transformed into a perpetual abider.

The Savior alluding to it said to his disciples that on the condition of their keeping his commandments He would come into them and take up His abode with them.

The experience unquestionably came to Paul, who says that it pleased God after He had called him by His grace to "reveal his Son in me." We all know that the occurrence near Damascus was not an inward, but an outward, revelation of Christ. The reference is evidently to something which transpired at a later period. The blessed secret is that there is a precious, beautiful experience for the child of God. It is for them that fear him. Sinners do not fear God. The Bible says so. There is, then, a holy secret to be imparted to the Christian if he is willing to accept.

There are several facts about the matter which impress the writer.

One is, that it is the secret of the Lord.

This explains why we can not make it clear to those who have it not. If a certain man has a secret, no one else but himself can tell it. People may guess what it is, but can not know assuredly until he is pleased to declare it.

This simple fact applied to the spiritual life will at once explain what has often puzzled the sanctified man. Filled with the blessing, yet he is unable of, and by himself, to make the experience clear to one who has it not.

Letters are written, sermons preached, books loaned, and conversations are held in vain. The face fails to light up with appreciation, and the mind to grasp the meaning of what has been said. The sanctified man thought that all he had to do was to run home and tell his family, rush around to his church and pastor and proclaim it, and all would immediately see, agree, be glad, and seek and find. To his amazement the countenances of his hearers remained heavy and cloudy, while some were grieved, and still others displeased. He told them carefully how he had obtained the blessing, and thought they would follow him; explained what it did for the soul, and supposed they would understand. To his surprise and sorrow they did neither one nor the other, and he was left to marvel.

If he had remembered the Scripture he would not have been astonished at the result. God had prepared him for the disappointment in the words, "I will give him a white stone, and in the white stone a new name written, which no man knoweth saving he that receiveth it." And still again in the words, "The secret of the Lord." It is the Lord's hidden truth, and it takes him to reveal it.

A second fact is, that there is a certain attitude or position needful to secure a secret.

When one concludes to repose a confidence in another, he draws the proposed confidant aside and whispers, while the one thus trusted bends the head and gives undivided attention to the utterance which a little distance makes inaudible.

So in securing this secret from the Lord, it is not to be obtained in a careless way. There is the drawing aside from the crowd, and an attitude of the soul which corresponds to what is seen when we behold the bent head, rapt face, and fixed attention of the hearer to all that is being said.

Here again we see the failure of many Christians in the obtainment of the blessed experience. They do not observe the conditions which are inexorably demanded of those who would enter within the veil. It is not truer than if a man fails to draw near and listen intently to what is whispered to him in a noisy street, he fails to get the intended information; than, if a person neglects to wait in a certain manner upon God, he will never know the secret of the Lord, will never be wiser concerning the second work of grace in the soul. There are just as fixed laws in the spiritual as in the natural world. Happy is the man who obeys them. As a farmer does not and can not make a good crop by laziness or an accident, so men do not rise and shine in the character world, are not caught up into great heights of the love and knowledge of God, by a stumbling chance or by waiting with listless eyes and idle hands for something to happen.

If the soul would see deep into the mysteries of heaven and grace, the vision will not come in a haphazard way. The wonderful experience of Daniel cost him weeks of lonely prayer and fasting on the banks of the river Hiddekel. It took all that was meant in the words "exiled to Patmos" to open the heavens to John. The baptism with the Holy Ghost and fire came at the end of ten days of ardent prayer and patient, faithful waiting on God in an upper room, away from the busy streets and talking circles of Jerusalem.

A man who prays three or four hours daily, is felt by others to be ahead in some important particulars. The preacher who has been on his knees an hour in humble, tearful waiting on God, begins in his sermon, not with his audience, but beyond and above them in tenderness of heart, clearness of spiritual vision, and conscious strength of soul; moreover, the audience feels it.

Look where we will, the faithful working of this spiritual law is beheld. He who turns aside sees the flaming bush, and talks with God. He who waits on the Lord renews his strength, and mounts up on eagle's wings. He who wraps the mantle about his head at the entering in of the cave and listens, will hear the still, small voice. And he who will lay all on the altar, and patiently, believingly, and prayerfully look upward, will be rewarded by the descending fire of the Holy Ghost, and the blessed secret of the Lord.

It is simply absurd for a man to say there is no such secret, when he refuses to comply with the conditions of obtaining the revelation, and it is lost time on our part to listen to their ridicule, arguments, doubts, and denials.

A third fact connected with the secret of the Lord

is the remarkable effect it has upon the person who has been put in its possession and enjoyment.

The writer has seen an individual tell another a secret, and instantly saw the face light up, a pleased look or smile overspread the countenance, and an almost indescribable expression spring in the eye, that came from the consciousness of a new and valued possession.

So we have been impressed with the people of God who obtained this secret. It was their smiling looks, shining faces, and speaking eyes that first deeply impressed us with the distinctiveness and superiority of the gift of grace they were enjoying.

The hard lines of the face had been changed into curves of pleasing repose; the lips, even when not speaking, seemed to declare inward rest; the eyes had a quiet, sunny look, like unto deep, clear springs; and the voice possessed a note of gladness, and at times an exultant ring, which impressed the dullest spiritual hearer.

It was the beaming light and joy of this secret which made the Irish gaze fascinated on Fletcher's face, when they did not understand a word that he uttered. They said there was heaven in the man's countenance.

Such a beautiful look the writer, when a young preacher, saw on the face of a lady who had been an invalid seventeen years. For all that weary time she had sat in a large chair, and crippled and stiffened with rheumatism, unable to do anything to help herself or others, quietly waited for death to relieve her from her acute sufferings. Six years were added to the seventeen, and still, with a patient smile on her lips, and that holy restful light in her face, she waited for God to say it was enough and call her home. Of the hundreds who visited her, all marked the pure, unearthly joy which filled her, and that was not only seen in the eye, and heard in the voice, but felt in her presence. The secret of the Lord kept her not only uncomplaining, but joyful through a quarter of a century of suffering.

She finally died, and they buried her, sitting in her invalid chair, which she had transformed into a throne, and in which she had ruled over many hearts as a crowned queen among the daughters of God. She died with the sweet, old-time smile on her lips, and was buried with it still resting on her face. There she is under the ground to-day, sitting in her throne-chair, and waiting for the coming of her Lord, whose voice will make her spring from the dust to meet him in the air, and whose blessed secret kept her strong, patient, and victorious through many years of as great pain and sore trouble as almost ever fell to the lot of any of God's children.

VIII.

WITHOUT REPUTATION.

THE writer once confounded reputation with character in the religious life. The two are very different. Reputation is what men think of us, and character is what we are in the sight of God. The first is what we appear to be; the second is what we really are. The one is a pleasant possession, but not essential; the other is blessed, and we must have it to stand before and live with God. We draw some reflections from the Scriptural words, "of no reputation."

One is, that it is possible to have reputation without character.

This springs from the fact that people can not read one another's hearts, and are ignorant of each other's lives. The public life may be one thing, and the private life another. A man may have a street face and a home face, and the two not agree. As the story goes, he may be a salmon in his own community, and a codfish in a distant city where he has not a single acquaintance. The countenance may be affable, the words pleasant, and the thoughts dark and foul.

Hence it is that people are in high places to-day

who would not be if they were known. The Bible prepares us for great shocks of surprise at the Day of Judgment, where reputation shall be utterly ignored, and character alone shall be demanded. Now and then sudden exposures in public and social life furnish us brief but powerful commentaries on these solemn allusions of the Scripture.

A lady was once speaking to me about her dead husband, saying that he detested hypocrites, and was filled with a spirit of honesty and honor himself. And yet we knew, and had the proof, of her husband being a petty thief. Only a few of us possessed the circumstance, and kept it secret. The man's ardent denunciations of sin sounded very oddly to the little group who really knew him. The community did not know. He died with a good reputation, but without the character many supposed he had. A life superstructure had been erected without a foundation.

At another time a prominent lady, apologizing to us for her husband's absence from Church, said, "But he is ripe for heaven."

We brooded over the speech of this unsuspecting woman, and it actually became oppressive as we remembered that not less than a dozen people possessed facts which were sufficient to blight and blast her marital happiness forever.

Great will be the astonishment of families,

Churches, communities, and multitudes on the Day of Days, when the real man and woman are brought to light, and God shows the difference between reputation and character.

Again, it is possible to have character without reputation.

Paul tells us that Christ had none, that he was "of no reputation." The same fact is brought out in his reference to the disciples of the Lord. The Savior himself said that all manner of evil should be spoken about them; they would be cast out of synagogues and put to death; and people in visiting those things upon them would think they were doing God service.

No one can question the fact of their possession of religious character, and yet they were without reputation.

So was Luther in his day, and Wesley in his time: they were jeered, ridiculed, denounced, and persecuted all through life; the churches were closed to them; ministers and magistrates united to condemn and oppose them; and yet they were men filled with the Holy Ghost, died in the faith, and went to heaven. These facts ought to bring many of God's servants great comfort to-day. Shut out from Churches, discounted in certain social and ecclesiastical circles, struck at and condemned in religious and secular papers, yet it is possible to have not only a conscience without offense, but to be the temple of the Holy Ghost and filled with the fullness of God. It is possible to have one's stock very low on earth, and that same religious stock be very high in heaven. It is possible to possess a pure heart, a genuine Christian character, and yet have the Church, as we see it in some places to-day, ashamed and afraid of us, and downright opposed to us.

So, just as one can have reputation without character, this strange, old world furnishes the equally remarkable spectacle of a person having character without any reputation.

Again, it is possible to have no reputation, and still be happy.

The fact is, it is very hard to be happy in a continuous way with what is termed a reputation. We have studied the cases of orators, musicians, authors, and all kinds of celebrities and prominent folks, and we have discovered that, as a rule, they are the uneasiest of people. A man with a reputation on his hands has an elephant to take care of. So much for its cumbersomeness. Again, it reminds me of an invalid, a baby at night, and a costly pet, all three in one. It needs a vast amount of attention, and in its exactions is perfectly tyrannical. It matters not how well its possessor "spoke his piece" before, he must excel, and more than excel every time, and delight and astonish everybody, or the man is gloomy, irritable, and miserable.

Apply this spirit to the ministerial, ecclesiastical, oratorical, or any other kind of reputation, and behold the result. I knew a man once whose great pride as a preacher was in having answered the roll-call of his Conference over thirty years without a single break. To have failed on the thirty-third time would have given him as much anguish as the commission of a sin. It was a kind of annual misery with him.

A layman boasted that he had sat forty years in one place in the church. He had also remained in the same spot in other respects. His pride took hold of the first fact. Here was his reputation. For any one even to attempt to take his seat angered him. His reputation cost him a good deal of mental peace, as all frequently saw.

There is a kind of pseudo-religious reputation born of the fact of years of church attendance, identification with various kinds of Church work, a cordial reception in the best ecclesiastical circles, and a standing well with Church functionaries and prominent people. This, like the rest, is filled with disquietude, and demands to be recognized, petted, patted, and generally coddled, smiled upon, and praised. It is full of fears of losing its peculiar ground, and others taking its place. To lay all this on the altar is one of the hardest of spiritual performances, and is the explanation why so few of that class of Christians obtain the blessing of sanctification.

Just a glance over the list hastily given is sufficient to convince the thoughtful that to get rid of reputation would be a relief all around, especially to the man who has groaned under the burden for months or years.

The fact is, that the happiest people the writer ever knew were those who had lost all they had in this line. With this loss had gone Church patronage, social honor, a certain kind of public reverence and attention, together with the estimation formerly entertained of their good sense and general levelheadedness. And yet these same people were bubbling over continually with a joy beyond all language to describe. All sanctified people have had third and seventh heaven experiences here, and it is with difficulty that we restrain our pen at this point.

Still again, it is possible to have no reputation, and be very useful.

We sometimes wonder that so many overlook the remarkable truth that the individuals who have wrought most spiritual good for this world, had no ecclesiastical reputation during their lives. It was after they were dead that their detractors and opposers took time to read what they had written and observe their works, and then the world saw that angels had been in their midst, and they knew it not; that God himself had spoken to them through human lips, and they had failed to know and receive him.

It does not require reputation to achieve great things for humanity. The Bible proves this in the record of the disciples, and history confirms the thought in the deeds of Luther, Wesley, Booth, and a host of others. The fact is, that reputation seems to be in the way of workers. It clogs, cumbers, hinders, embarrasses, paralyzes, and in many ways keeps one from doing for God, and especially doing his best for God.

It is well to have nothing to distract and absorb us when Christ calls us to labor for him; it is well to have both hands empty for him. If we have other gods and idols of our own, even though that idol be only reputation, we will never be and do for the Savior what he desires. Such a man can not afford to speak at every providential call because he has an oratorical fame to support and perpetuate; or another person will not engage in mission or slum work because a certain social prestige is lost by such a life. So the soul-stirring and life-saving message was not delivered, and the diamond in the gutter was not found and lifted up.

We know of a city where there are seven missions, and they are all run by people who have lost their ecclesiastical or Church reputation. Not a denomination in the place, nor all the denominations combined, have been sufficient to run a single mission; and yet here is a body of people laughed at, despised, and in a sense ostracized and tabooed, running seven distinct works.

A concluding thought is this, that there is going to be a great revolution of opinion and judgment at the Last Day.

People who stood very high on the earth will stand very low before the Bar of Christ when all hearts shall be known. A great many "big men," so-called in this world, will be found to be exceedingly small under the marvelous light of eternity. The sudden shrinkage of individuals who were admired, quoted, and even feared on earth, will occasion one of the most shocking sensations of the Judgment-day. Men will never cease to talk about those dreadful collapses and downfalls, and which were long ago predicted by Christ under the figure of the house built on a foundation of sand.

On the other hand, some people who were overlooked, or who were discounted, despised, laughed at, and rejected, will loom up in such moral grandeur, such mighty proportions of spiritual attainment, that the astonishment will be even greater here than the amazement already described.

We knew quite a wealthy man who recently died. He was a member of the Methodist Episcopal Church, South. Out of a large fortune he gave thirty dollars a year to the support of the Church, and was bitterly opposed to missions, especially those in the foreign field. Yet this man had a great ascendency in his Church. Perhaps court was paid to him because of what was hoped he might yet do. But he did nothing. He died without doing anything. The outside world did not, and does not, know the littleness of his Christian and Church life. They were much impressed with his imposing form and rolling guttural speech. They thought he was a pillar in the Church, when he was only a sleeper. They imagined that he supported the Church, when he only occasionally entertained the bishops.

The sight of this man shrinking, drawing in, drawing up, drying up, and generally going to nothing under the solemn, silent, searching gaze of the Son of God will be one of the sickening and horrifying visions of the Day of Judgment.

The writer is acquainted with a woman who, filled with the Holy Ghost and burning up with the love of souls, started with her slender means a little mission in one of our large cities. She was ridiculed, slandered, and struck at in many ways. She bore all silently and patiently, founded a Sabbath-school of fifty children picked up from the street, and with her simple revival services among people who never went to Church, saw twenty clear conversions in three months. This was not a large number, but it happened to be a larger average than that of a large Church of several million members, which reported sixteen thousand conversions for one year's work. The denomination referred to has seventeen thousand preachers on its roll; so there were a thousand preachers who did not have a single convert. As for the three million members, according to figures, they did nothing. The woman I referred to brought twenty souls to Christ in three months. As examined in a comparative way, her work begins to grow upon one. Then, when we remember what the Savior said about the worth of a soul, her achievement was great indeed. In addition, when we notice that in the line of soul-saving she did the work of eighty preachers, the whole thing, in a strange, solemn way, prepares us for the astounding scenes of the Day of Reward and Doom.

Aladdin saw a small copper lamp or vessel lying on the seashore near him. As he looked upon it a thread of smoke began ascending from the vessel, and spreading and enlarging until it became a great cloud, and then assumed the shape of a gigantic geni. After a while the shape disappeared, the cloud of smoke returning with steadily diminishing proportions to the diminutive metal lamp at Aladdin's feet.

The fictitious scene becomes all powerful when applied to the occurrences at the Judgment. So will we see the swagger, strut, puff, and swell of a mere reputation steadily disappear before our eyes. It may once have filled the land and overshadowed thousands; and now behold! It is lost in a poor, morally shriveled creature who cowers at the feet of Christ.

And, thank God! we shall also see the other sight. We will behold coming forth to public view from some humble, despised, and wronged one of earth, the beauty, grace, glory, dignity, and majesty of a Christ-like nature and life. It can be hidden and kept down and shut in no longer. It is God's own work wrought in the face of Satanic hate and every human discouragement. It is something to rejoice over and to praise God for. And it is a piece of justice done to suffering man as well. And so the glory of that life, so long bound in with hardship and thrust into obscurity, shall stream forth at last, and fill the firmament of observation.

IX.

THE COMFORT IN TEMPTATION.

TEMPTATION is anything but a joyous experience. Whether it is realized as a cloud upon the spirit, or a violent attack upon faith and love, or an assault through the appetites, it is something which no Christian desires. It is a moral necessity in this world, so we are told, and believe, and also discover; but we are not the less delighted that in heaven we will feel its power no more forever.

As temptation is a heavy-hearted experience, the caption of this article, "Comfort in Temptation," would strike the reader at first as contradictory. But one is as true as the other; in fact, the apostle tells us to count it all joy when we fall into divers temptations. So the two can go together; we can be in heaviness through manifold trials of this kind, and yet be joyful.

We, however, are not referring in this article to the joy of which St. James speaks. The "Comfort" we are writing about springs from other facts, and we are glad to bring such consolation to those who are tempted and tried by the great adversary of their souls.

The first comfort is clearly stated in the Bible in the words, "There hath no temptation taken you but such as is common to man."

If there is not strength and consolation in this declaration to the tried soul, then we know nothing about human nature. To be lost in a vast wilderness is a paralyzing experience; but to see signs of human life here and there would immediately cause hope to spring up in the heart, and strength into the limb. The successful climber of the dizzy heights of the Matterhorn brought a great company of people to do what otherwise they never would have had the nerve to have accomplished. After Columbus had gone across the dreaded Atlantic, and thereby dissipated its superstitious terrors, there came a host of adventurers on his track with great cheerfulness and assurance. The moral effect of having been preceded by another in some line of toil and difficulty is tremendous. What man has done and endured can be borne and accomplished again by man. This is the reasoning of men, and the very thought is inspiration and life itself.

This is the same principle of comfort embraced in the statement that the dark, sad temptations of life which try us so severely are not peculiar to us, but are common to man. Others have wrestled with and conquered these things of the spiritual life which are now dismaying us; others have trod these deserts, or plowed these seas, and found a San Salvador beyond. In spite of long sailing there has been land, and landing, and coming forth, and victory for others, and the same can be for us.

The desolate state of the heart; the lonely, friendless feeling of the soul; the wave of sickening doubt; the suggestion that friends have ceased to love you, that health will fail, and usefulness cease, and the poorhouse be at last your refuge—all these are influences and whispers which the accuser of God and of his brethren has injected into many a faithful heart that is now in rapture near the throne, striking a golden harp or waving a palm of eternal victory.

Under temptation, one's rapturous feelings go down; so did those of the holy Madame Guyon. A great fear arises as to divine deliverance from trouble; the saintly Payson went through the same experience. The heart sinks for a while under a lonely trial; so did Paul, who, when he met friends at last at the Three Taverns, "thanked God and took courage."

The most pious and influential preacher in one of our Southern States said that once for fully thirty minutes he was conscious of a violent inward urging to be profane. He said his soul recoiled in horror from it, that he recognized the dark influences as the work of the devil, but that the distressing movement was there, nevertheless.

The thought of suicide as an escape from sickness and trouble is purely Satanic, and yet it has come to the best of people, who have resisted it with proper promptness and disapproval, knowing full well it came from Satan, and that it stood for a sin which, from its very nature, was unpardonable.

It is certainly a great mental relief in the midst of sore experiences, when Satan would have us believe they are peculiar to us, thereby making us feel we are the worst of all God's creatures—I say it is blessed to the soul to hear God's Word affirming, "There hath no temptation taken you but such as is common to man." Such a statement upon the part of heaven is bound to bring the sweetest consolation to the soul.

A second comfort in temptation is found in the words that, "God is faithful, who will not suffer you to be tempted above that ye are able."

According to these words there is no excuse for men who fall under temptation. The temptation was not greater than they could have borne. This is God's own declaration, and we believe God.

Those who go down under the assault of the Evil One, invariably begin to whine and whimper about it, saying they could not help it; that the assault was of such a nature that they could not resist; that they were, so to speak, overpowered. But the Bible says they do not tell the truth, that they fell with a superior force in them. They went down before something weaker than themselves. A man has fallen under the blow of a boy's hand! Let us read the Word of God again, "God is faithful, who will not suffer you to be tempted above that ye are able." So, then, according to this, they could have endured the attack.

This same statement, which puts the fall of the Christian in a new light, also fills the tempted but as yet unfallen child of God with great comfort. There is no need to fall. Greater is He that is in us, than the devil and the world outside of us. The powers of darkness will be held in check; they will not be allowed to do their worst upon us. The winds and waves of hell will be weighed and gauged by the Divine Hand before they are allowed to beat upon His servant. In a word, there is no necessity for spiritual foundering and shipwreck.

Under the light of this clear Bible statement down go the timeworn excuses for falling in "the smell of the wine at the Lord's table," "the odor of a saloon," "the power of habit," "the force of suggestion," "the influence of a smile," "the touch of a hand," etc.

Under this jubilee blast of liberty we can go as free men past saloons, be delivered from habit, keep strong under look and touch of evil, and be more than conquerors through Him who loved us.

A third comfort in temptation is declared in the words, "He will with the temptation also make a way to escape." Here is something more than strength to endure promised; it is actual deliverance and escape.

There are several ways in which God can deliver us from the hour and power of temptation.

One is by the removal of the object.

This we do not believe is frequently done, as our probation, from the nature of the case, demands that we be morally tested and tried. So to put us on trial, and then remove the very class and character of things which will declare and reveal us, would be to act contradictorily, and, indeed, absurdly. If we are not tempted and tried, there can be no Day of Rewards for us. Still there are times when God, who knows how much we can endure, will remove the object that under present conditions might be too powerful for us, and allow it to come later to the attack, when we are better prepared.

Again He delivers us by urging His tempted follower to a precipitate flight.

Time was when we regarded a man's avoidance of a place of moral danger, and withdrawal from certain social surroundings as a confession of weakness and an indication of cowardice. But with the flight of years we became convinced that such a course was proof, not only of the wisdom, but of moral courage as well.

Flight in some instances is the best, truest, and safest thing we can do. Joseph achieved an immortal victory when he fled from his temptress. There are places and circumstances where we can not tarry or dally. To do so is to fall. The impulse or impression to fly is from God himself, who would thereby save us. The divine whisper has been unmistakable at times in the life when there was peril, and when God saw the danger was greater than the man dreamed. The inward voice was to "fly!" And many have obeyed, and fled, and so have been delivered, where others, under a mistaken idea of Christian hardihood and courage, have gone down.

We read in First Samuel that David asked the Lord, "Will the men of Keilah deliver me into the hands of Saul?" and God answered, "They will deliver thee up." This is a wonderfully impressive sentence, and shows God's knowledge of men embraces all that they are capable of doing, and what they will or would do under certain circumstances. This same Lord has lost none of his love for his people, and none of his knowledge of the sinful heart. So His whispers come to the soul as suddenly and clearly as ever warning was given to David, "If such and such a thing takes place, you will fall into sin."

No one can read certain warnings given by Wesley and others of the old writers on the line of discreetness and circumspectness of life, without realizing that they had come into strange experiences and had gathered wisdom as the years went by.

There is an instrument lately invented by which it is said the capacity of children for the strain and drain of school hours is tested. God needs no machine of any kind to know how much we can bear in the hour of moral trial. He knows us altogether. He is aware that a protracted assault upon the soul would cause some Christians to go down under certain circumstances, and so, as it does not agree with His plans to remove the cause, His method of deliverance to his child is the whisper to fly.

The third way God saves us in and from temptation, is by a mighty pouring of divine grace and power into the soul.

The effect of this is to so lift the Christian up above the influence of the tempting thing or being, that he marvels how he could ever have been so shaken and stirred. Under increased divine love and strength the whole matter looks so little and contemptible that he wonders how he could ever have been moved by such an ambition, pursuit, pleasure, or object.

This deliverance, considered in the light of reason,

is like a man struggling to lift a two-hundred-pound rock, when suddenly the power of two other men is added to him, and lo! off he walks with the boulder with the greatest ease. Or it is like a regiment sorely beset in battle, just able to hold its ground, when, with a great shout, a new regiment dashes to their aid, and now with a still greater cry the two bodies of troops charge and sweep the field before them.

In like manner there are "evil days," as Paul calls them, when we simply "stand" and "having done all to stand." God permits this for various reasons. The very ability to stand, however, is victory in itself, and a divine rescue; but God has a greater deliverance still, and a much more marvelous victory. After that we have suffered awhile, he will pour down reenforcements from the skies in the shape of brigades and divisions of spiritual joy and power, and with a shout of triumph we will charge over everything and plant our triumphant banners upon the loftiest forts and strongest citadels of our spiritual enemies.

It is as though the strength of three men had been given to one. It is the arrival of the second regiment to help the first. It is the bringing up of the reserve corps, which had been held in watchful observation of us, and at the critical moment was sent rushing and flashing into the heart and life, and lo!

the hour, field, battle was ours, through Jesus Christ our Lord.

The victory is so great that the Bible says we are "more than conquerors." We not only have a rock to kill Goliath, but several other stones are placed in the wallet, or scrip, in case that if more giants should come along we could slay, not only one monster, but, under the mighty grace of God, destroy the whole breed. It is a superabundant victory.

This is like God. This is the way He deals with His people who are faithful to Him. He not only will not give us over to the will of our enemies, but will, according to David, lift our heads up above our enemies. He has not only saved us in the past; but we can say with Paul concerning the future, "The Lord will deliver me from every evil work, and will preserve me unto His heavenly kingdom."

X.

THE FOUR LOOKS TOWARD SODOM.

SODOM, with its natural beauty, sin, vileness, foulness, God-forgetfulness, and heaven-defiance, is a good type of the world. Upon this beautiful, wicked, and doomed city four different looks were cast by four different beings. They stand for truths of a solemn and all-important nature. One day in my Bible reading, I was suddenly impressed with this steady gazing of individuals at this city of the plain, and the mind as immediately associated and connected the looks with the truths we have alluded to.

The first look was cast by Lot.

It was the gaze of a man who was getting his own consent to live there. He was well aware of the character of the place, and yet looked with longing in the gaze. According to the Bible he ought not to have dreamed of abiding in such a place. The blessedness of walking not with the ungodly, standing not with sinners, and sitting not with the scornful, did not begin with the Psalmist's time; but, as a duty and necessity, commenced with the first century of the world's history. Can a man take fire in his bosom and be unburned, and handle pitch and be undefiled?

Lot's going to Sodom to live meant the corruption and destruction of his entire family. So much do association and surroundings mean in this world. And yet people, without a thought, make changes and moves of various character that are certain to affect disastrously their own household for time and eternity.

Sin begins with a look in forbidden directions. So Eve fixed her eyes on the interdicted fruit, and David from the roof of his palace gazed one evening where he should not. So, while we sing there is life for a look, there is also death from a look.

It is remarkable how evil will come in like a tide if the first glance deepens into a gaze. The only hope is to make a covenant with the eyes, and say, "I will not look on any wicked thing."

It is also curious and significant to see how Lot got into Sodom. It was not at a bound; but he first "looked toward Sodom," then "journeyed toward Sodom;" later still, "he pitched his tent over against Sodom," and finally found himself in Sodom. Each successive step was doubtless attended with additional gazing; but the first look witnessed the start to the unholy place.

Some one says there are two ways of getting down from a tower; one is to jump off, and the other to come down by the steps. So there is a way of going rapidly with a single leap into sin and ruin; but very few take that route. The great majority come down by the steps, by the successive stages of moral lapse typified in the expressions, "looking toward," "journeying in the direction," and "pitching the tent over against Sodom."

The thing to do is to avoid the first look, and if that has been cast, to say, "I will look no more."

Once, when riding along a country road, I saw a bird charmed by a snake. The reptile lay full length on the limb of a tree, and had its eyes fixed on its spellbound victim, not a foot away. The bird, with extended, tremulous wings, and low, distressed cry, had its head bent forward, and was gazing into the red, open mouth and glistening eyes of its ensnarer and would-be destroyer. I got down from my horse, and with a large stick killed the serpent and rescued the almost exhausted songster of the woods; but the scene actually produced a kind of heart nausea, and I never forgot the impression.

The lesson is not to let the eye get on the world, lest the eyes of the world get fixed on you, with its basilisk, destructive gaze, and there would be no deliverance.

The second look directed upon Sodom was by the Lord.

I know of no scene in the Bible that is more impressive than this, in which we see the Almighty standing on the brow of the mountains which skirt the valley of Siddim, and looking silently and fixedly upon Sodom as it lay in its wealth, beauty, wickedness, and utter corruption in the center of the plain.

As the people sinned on that day, how little they dreamed it was their last, and that God in human form was standing on a mountain ten miles away, looking down upon them! It was a look of sorrow, condemnation, and judgment. What thoughts must have rolled through the Divine mind at this hour! He had given the people a beautiful land, and every material blessing, and time in which to save themselves and honor God, and yet they had misused everything, perverted his gifts, despised his grace, broken his laws, rejected his warnings, ill-treated his servants and messengers, and put themselves finally beyond the pale of mercy.

It is a fearful thought that a person may live such a life as to bring upon him or her the silent and fixed look of God. The dreadfulness of the thought is, that such a gaze means that judgment is close by.

The third look thrown upon Sodom was by Lot's wife.

She had been mercifully drawn by angel hands out of the doomed city, and was in a place of safety. The command given to her was not to look back, which is the command to the pardoned and regenerated soul until to-day. The woman disobeyed, and, turning, fixed her eyes upon the burning city. The awful picture had scarcely been made upon the retina of the eye, when she was as instantly destroyed and turned to a pillar of salt.

The disposition to look back on the world we have left, and the sinful life we have forsaken, is one of the strange facts we have to encounter in the spiritual life. The hymn-book recognizes it in the words, "Prone to wander, Lord, I feel it; prone to leave the God I love." We are called to deal with it as a principle in the moral life, and know it to exist in spite of the teachings of modern theology. It is the explanation of many strange things we see in the Church, and accounts for the cases of spiritual petrifaction we find in the pulpit and pew.

One would think that a regenerated heart would gladly push on to mountains of a higher grace and deliverance, even as the angel told Lot and his family, "Stay not in all the plain; escape for thy life to the mountains." What is there in the old life to tempt us again? What is there in Sodom to draw us back?

And yet, in spite of Zindendorf and all his followers; in spite of an army of smaller writers, there is this disposition in the regenerated soul to look back, and, worse still, the inclination becomes an act. As a consequence the ghastly miracle of people being turned to stone is still going on. We see it in faces and lives. Men and women once sweeping across the plains of salvation are now stationary, and become like adamant. The people not only see it, but they themselves feel it. Faces of stone in the pew, faces of stone in the official board, and faces of stone in the pulpit! We can not always tell when the backward look was turned, and what special thing or object occasioned it; but we all can see the life suddenly arrested, and the face of stone looking from the stationary life upon us.

The fourth look on Sodom was cast by Abraham.

He stood on the mountains next day, and saw the destruction which God had sent on the cities of the plain. The Bible says that the Lord rained fire upon them from out of heaven, and the smoke went up as the smoke of a great furnace. The spectacle must have been horrifying beyond all words to describe. To see a country which the day before was all beautiful and prosperous, with bustling cities, and teeming with multitudes of people, suddenly ingulfed in fire, and literally swept with cyclones of flame and smoke, and, underneath it all, to catch glimpses of what was transpiring, was truly a scene of horror, and well calculated to fix the gaze of not only one man, but every eye that could endure the sight.

This look was not mentioned without a purpose. It is not less certain that one part of the human family will, from the heights of eternity, behold the overthrow and witness the destruction of this world. They will see the flames licking up cities, forests, and rivers alike, and leaping from the mountain-tops like wild animals. They will see whirlwinds of fire sweeping about like cyclones on the plains, vast pillars of smoke now appearing like waterspouts, and now seen falling here and there like great pillars under the touch of a Samson hand. Complete and overwhelming will be the ruin of terrestrial things on that day.

There was no joy in Abraham's look that morning of disaster to Sodom, and there will be nothing of the kind in the heart of God's people on the dreadful Day of Judgment. But there will be no dissent to, or disapproval of, the divine proceedings in that fearful hour. It will all come to the silent witnesses in that time, that it was in vain God loaded the people down with material bounties; in vain for them harvests waved, flowers and fruits abounded, flocks and herds multipled, cities prospered and Plenty waved her wand over the broad earth. It was in vain God gave his Son, sent his Spirit, and filled the earth with churches, bibles, and preachers. It was in vain he bore with them, and warned and promised and pleaded ten thousand times. They would not have him to reign over them. They mocked at message and messenger. They broke every commandment, grieved the Holy Ghost, and trampled the blood of Christ under their feet as an unholy thing. They laid up wrath against the Day of Wrath. They made themselves ripe for destruction. And it has come at last. This is the end long foretold by prophet and affirmed by God. Time is ended. The earth is being burned up; the heavens are passing away; the nations who forgot God, and still can not pray, are calling for the mountains to fall upon them; and from the great cliffs of the eternal world, the Redeemed stand and view the dreadful scene. The typical look of Abraham is fulfilled at last.

XI.

THE STRENGTH OF SAMSON.

AS far as it is possible for a doctrine or great spiritual truth to be illustrated in a man, God has striven to show heavenly facts in vessels of clay.

Notably is this seen in the case of Samson. The marvelous strength given the man, and his use of the same, was intended to teach something; and if that teaching is not holiness and some of its striking features, then the wonderful life of the man is still an unsolved problem.

Accepting the thought that holiness is thus typified and taught, and at once Samson's life becomes luminous and full of profound instruction as well as warning to us. The reader is called upon to observe several facts.

First, the man was a Nazarite.

The Nazarites were the typical holy people. They were under peculiar vows to God, and lived a life of self-denial and sacrifice. They drank no wine, ate no grapes, and were not allowed to cut their hair.

A sanctified man is the Nazarite of to-day. He is under peculiar vows, and is expected to be different from his regenerated brethren. Things which are lawful in themselves and may be practiced or enjoyed by others, are not allowed to him. There are books he can not read, and songs he can not sing, and pleasures and pursuits from which he is precluded by God and man. The unshorn hair and refraining from grapes and wine stand for principles of life and conduct, which will make a peculiar and holy people. The Nazarite in early days, and now, was highly exalted; great was to be his honor; but not less true is the fact that he had to walk a very narrow and lonely path. It costs to be a Nazarite.

Another fact about Samson's life was that his strength was the gift of God.

So is holiness the direct work of the Lord upon the soul. He imparts it. It can come in no other way.

An additional fact was that the marvelous strength of the man was a secret.

The fact of the general ignorance as to where his power lay is seen in the credulity and blunders of Delilah. No one connected it with his hair. When Samson told his betrayer that if seven green withes were used to bind him, he would be helpless, she believed him. So in regard to the pinning of his head to the wall. The woman who knew him best did not dream where his mighty power lay.

All this is significant. It means that the unction and influence of the sanctified man is a mystery to all who have it not. They see the effects, but do not know how to account for it. Often they say it is personal magnetism, eloquence, a pleasing manner, and many other like things. The real secret is hidden from them. The white stone with the new name is only known by those who have received it.

A fourth fact connected with the history is, that it was not necessary for Samson to be a physical giant to possess his strength.

We doubt not that he was a man of ordinary size, and very likely below the average stature of men. This fact alone would actually add to the wonder of this human miracle, and so to the glory of God.

We recall once hearing a magnificent female voice in a large church. It was so deep, rich, and powerful, that we turned to look at the singer, and saw a frail-looking little woman that a mere touch or jostle seemed able to push into the grave; and yet from the delicate creature came pouring forth the full rich sounds that were thrilling and moving everybody.

Doubtless, the physical frame of Samson seemed utterly inadequate to do the deeds which he performed. It must have perfectly astonished the people to see him rip great massive gates from the city wall, and carry them with ease miles away; or to see him destroy a lion or achieve any one of the remarkable exploits for which he was famous. The things done were so disproportionate to his size, they so towered above him according to the natural eye, that the miracle was declared in the performance, and God was seen and glorified.

We have beheld the blessing of sanctification come upon and shine forth from apparently very unpromising subjects. Not to speak of men who were pigmies in body but giants in spiritual power, we have also been made to wonder at the marvelous divine enduement abiding in individuals who were rough in appearance, unattractive in person, unpolished in speech, and without education or culture whatever. They were not even remarkable for gifts, and so were not giants of any kind. They were plain, unpretending men and women, and this very fact brought out the power and glory of God all the more. The extraordinary was seen plainly against a background of the ordinary.

A fifth fact relative to the strength of Samson was that it would arise in him in mightiest force at certain times.

While he always had the secret of strength, yet there were occasions when this power would fairly boil in him, and rush forth like the sweep of an irresistible tempest. Once this happened at the sight of a lion; again as he looked at the gates of Gaza; and still again on viewing a multitude of Philistines. According to the Scripture, the Spirit would come upon him, and with his blood rushing through his veins, his muscles swelling like great ropes, and a shout of triumph ringing from his lips, Samson would hurl himself upon the enemy, and there would be a marvelous victory.

All this is perfectly familiar to the sanctified man; that strange coming upon him of the Spirit, and the feeling that he can not only leap over a wall, but run through a troop, strangle lions, tear up gates of brass, and scatter a host of the king's enemies anywhere, everywhere, and every time.

It seemed, when the Divine energy would surge through Samson, that he had to throttle, tear up or knock down something. This same peculiar force swells in the soul of the sanctified, and brings with it a sense of physical power that is felt all over the body. If sin was in a material form before the man of God at such a time, it would have to go down. The hands reach out instinctively to shatter and destroy the works of the devil.

So when once the writer beheld a preacher shaking with the power of God upon him, cast something afar with his hand, and with a quick sweep of the foot hurl some wooden object from the platform, we knew how he felt, and what he meant, and what was in him. We knew that an overplus of spiritual force was working out in a physical way, and that he had thus to relieve himself, even as Samson, heaven filled and fired, felt compelled to tear up heavy gates, pack them for miles, and pitch them on the top of a hill.

Many times the writer has felt this strange influence as he stood in the pulpit. It would fill the soul and fairly tingle to the ends of the body. It was an intoxication that did not interfere with, but brought clearheadedness. A thrilling joyous sense of power throbbed through the entire being, and the hands fairly itched to upheave gates, choke lions, pull down walls, and beat a triumphant way through every kind of difficulty and opposition.

We do not doubt that when the Spirit of the Lord would come upon Samson, he would shout, and under his tremendous onset nothing could stand before him. In like manner we have seen the holy power filling and overflowing some servant of God. While the blessing is always a resident latent strength, yet at the sight of a spiritual foe, a work to be done, a battle to fight, and a victory to win, this wondrous spiritual force will be felt coming down on brain, heart, and body, as well as springing up from the very depths of the soul, and the man will stand before us filled, glowing, and fairly transfigured.

It is noticeable by every one that if the possessor of the blessing is true to God, the Lord will never leave him in the presence of his enemies without this divine girding and anointing. Sometimes the man will have gone through the preparatory services and is ready to rise with his text before a great audience, when suddenly he feels the sweet sense of power coming upon him. As he opens his lips and speaks, the volume increases, and in a little while a Samson of New Testament times, with his mysterious strength and perfect ability to meet the demand of the hour, is before us, and sweeping all things before him.

The writer has seen the power rising up and filling a man in the pulpit until all felt the strange, inscrutable presence of God in the speaker, and realized that a giant stood before us. And, moreover, he was a giant, had the strength of a giant, and did the work of a giant in the swaying at his will of a multitude of people. Samson was living again and at his old-time work.

We have seen this power fall upon a preacher when he was concluding a sermon. He had made his points, convinced the understanding of the people before him, had shown the vileness and helplessness of man, and declared the almighty ability of Christ to save and save to the uttermost. At this juncture we have seen the Spirit of the Lord descend upon the speaker, and then such a holy, rapturous, triumphant, ringing laugh would peal from his lips, that no words could describe the panic and consternation among sinners and backsliders. Such as had strength to move at all would rush to the altar and fall down, while others would be stricken into a silence that was both remarkable and awful. The God of Samson had come! Samson himself was again before us, his form actually appearing to tower above us, his voice echoing from church-walls as from mountain-sides, and the altar-floor seeming like another plain of Philistia covered with dead and wounded Philistines.

A sixth fact about Samson was that, when the power was upon him, any weapon he could lay his hand upon, was sufficient to win the victory.

For instance, at the time when he met the lion in the way, and the animal "roared against him," the Scripture says, "the Spirit of the Lord came mightily upon him, and he rent him as he would have rent a kid." But the same passage tells us that when he did this, "he had nothing in his hand."

At another time, a multitude of his enemies were arrayed before him. The crowd "shouted against him," but the Bible says, "The Spirit of the Lord came mightily upon him," and then adds that Samson found a bone lying on the ground, and, rushing into the combat with this simple weapon, he slew with it one thousand men.

It is to be noticed that the Spirit was upon him

when he did so much with those empty hands on one occasion and with a mere bone on the other.

All this is profoundly significant, and means that a man, with the blessing in him and filling him to overflowing, at the call of duty and trumpet-blast of battle can win victory with the simplest of means and instrumentalities.

We all know what it is to see great union-meetings of the Churches, with combined choirs, platform notables, rosetted ushers, artistic solos, eloquent prayers, and great discourses on the oratorical, logical, and theological order, and yet nothing accomplished. The chariots of Assyria had been hired, and the horses of Egypt secured, but victory did not come. Something seemed to be lacking. The Spirit of God had not and did not fall upon the services and the people.

Again, we all have seen the tremendous pulpit effort, and a series of tremendous efforts, utterly fail to do what was longed for and expected. The man was scholarly, polished, refined, and a christian at that. His logic was unanswerable, and his manner beyond criticism. He was an elegant christian gentleman, preaching the truth; but somehow God did not answer by fire. There was a perfect magazine of spiritual weapons, parks of pulpit artillery, some sky-rockets for signal service, cavalry charges of propositions, and admirable manipulation of the congregation, but nothing was done. There was no "power." The results of the meeting were more like that of a dress parade and review than an actual battle.

Over against all this let a man have the blessing we are writing about, and the fruit of his life and the result of his labors will at once begin to excite the talk and astonishment of the community and country at large. It will be observed that while he employs the usual methods and agencies of grace, yet he does not lean on them or look to them, but to something or somebody above and beyond. The "power" seems to come down in a way independent of people, circumstances, and everything. No matter what he says and what he does, a heavenly influence is at once felt in convicting, softening, quickening, comforting, and saving power. There seems to be a double response to what he utters, one from heaven and the other from the hearts of men. He is clothed with holy energy, and God owns, acknowledges, and honors his servant in ways most unmistakable from the skies.

It matters not whether he is empty-handed or full-handed, whether he gives a complete sermon or a simple talk,—the strong man of God is always before us, and never having a defeat. There are times when he may seem to have nothing in his hands, or he may have picked up a mere bone, and yet he, being filled with the Holy Ghost, sweeps everything before him.

The beautiful solo, sung with artistic grace and studied effect, has left every heart unmoved and every eye dry as stone, when under a single stanza or two of an old hymn, the man we speak of has every face bathed with tears. The eloquent prayer got nowhere, and the studied discourse was lost in thin air; but Samson, the real spiritual Samson, with whom God wants to fill the Church to-day, being present and called on to conclude, put his consecrated arms around the pillars of God's promises, and in a few broken, burning utterances of the soul, and with a mighty upheaving, pulling-down grasp of faith, fairly brought the heavens down, and he, Samson, and the people alike, were all covered up with shouts, cries, laughter, weeping, clapping of hands, and sweeping clouds of glory.

> "Our fathers had this power,
>   And we may have it too!
> 'T is the power, the power!
> 'T is the very same power!
> 'T is the power, the power!
> 'T is the power which Jesus
>   Promised should come down."

XII.

THE DEFEAT AT AI.

THE reader will remember that, after the children of Israel had crossed the Jordan into Canaan, and after the great victory at Jericho, there came a most mortifying defeat to them at a place called Ai. The aggravating features of the humiliation were the small size of the town assailed and the smaller number of the enemy's forces, compared to the Israelites. Well might the people be astounded.

The explanation of the reverse was, there had been transgression in the camp. God was grieved, and would not go out with his people to battle. As a result their power was gone, and they not only could do nothing with their foes, but could not even stand before them.

We read that Joshua rent his clothes and fell upon his face, while the elders of Israel put dust on their heads. It was after that, God told them there was an accursed thing in the camp. The search was made, and under the tent of Achan was found the wedge of gold and Babylonish garment which had been secreted there by the disobedient Israelite. The rest of the history is well known as to the stoning of

Achan, the destruction of the hidden things, and the burning up of all the man's property.

Once more power and victory returned to the children of Israel; God went out with their armies, and the nations melted at their very presence.

The occurrence makes a melancholy narrative, but it is something that has transpired many times since in the lives of Christians and in the history of Churches.

It is not uncommon to see a Church, after a career of usefulness and power, go into a condition of moral apathy and deadness. It is even more common to behold men, once clothed with heavenly zeal and mighty with the unction of God, gradually cool off, lose their spiritual force, and become weak like other men. They have had Jerichos to fall before them, but now, under some strange change, they can not take Ai. Indeed, they retire from before Ai. They recognize the loss in themselves, and others observe it as well. Something has happened. Something is the matter.

Time would fail to tell of preachers and laymen who ran well for a season, and then gradually or suddenly their triumphant career was ended. There have been a number of evangelists who fairly blazed for a while, and then their light began to wane and finally, in some instances, went out entirely. Among the names were some prominent ones. They had the ear of the people, drew multitudes, pulled down fire from heaven, and yet after all this went into eclipse and darkness.

In some cases there can be a proper explanation like unto that of John the Baptist, who saw himself decrease and Christ increase. The man's work may be ended, his mission accomplished, and so he passes away.

In other instances the explanation is not so easy. The demand for workers is great, the laborers are few, the people need instruction and salvation, and the sheep are scattered; why should men once so useful, become useless, and who shone as stars of the first magnitude retrograde to the glimmering of the fourth and fifth rank, and at last go out altogether? Surely the Holy Ghost did not exhaust Himself on them in their first year. Surely usefulness should increase with growing wisdom and experience and from long and deep communion with God. Certainly some kind of explanation is in order.

It is curious to hear the man himself talk. He tells of great battles in the past, great victories over every kind of forbidding circumstance. It is while lying in the fields besieging little Ai, he describes how he captured Jericho on the fourth or fifth day, his auditors meanwhile wondering why he can not take the small place now before him.

His explanations of present inability and failure are voluminous, some of them pathetic, others eloquent. He says that his natural force is abating. But it is noticed that he eats as much as ever, and perhaps more. He speaks of nervous prostration a great deal: time was, he had more to say about bodily prostration on the floor in prayer. It is sad to hear him talking so much about what "the doctors say about his case." Meantime the people are also discussing his case; but it is another one than that which the physicians are thinking about. One is looking at the physical and the other at the spiritual side of the man. From what he says about the great power he once possessed before he broke down physically, one would suppose that spiritual force could not abide in or proceed from a frail and delicate body; that religious influence depended more on health than grace, and on the state of the nerves rather than on the condition of the soul.

Without depreciating the advantages of health and strength in the work of God, yet, as an offset to this idea, we would call attention to Summerfield, Payson, and a number of others, who scarcely ever knew an hour of physical ease, who would in preaching be interrupted by hemorrhages, and swoon in the pulpit after an hour's faithful labor, and yet their power with God and man was marvelous.

Let it be understood that we are not referring to defeats before places which would not surrender if an angel fresh from heaven would come and offer them the gospel. The Bible speaks very plainly about individuals and places that are given over to idols and to believe a lie. Christ himself came to towns where He could do no mighty works, and Paul came to Athens, and had to leave it as he found it, in its silly mirth and with its multitudinous false gods. To this day there are Jerusalems that have to be wept over as not knowing the time of their visitation, and towns whose very dust, Christ says, shake off from your feet.

We allude not to defeats before such communities, but to the departure of spiritual power from individuals who once possessed it abundantly, and to needless reverses before Ai, when the place should and can be taken by men and women filled with the Holy Ghost. The town has not been given over to hardness, and yet it is not taken for God. What is the matter? There is an explanation. What is it?

Just as in the instance of Israel, something wrong had been done, and the wedge of gold and Babylonish garment were buried under a tent in the midst of the camp—so there has been a moral misstep, a transgression of the Divine law, and the fact is hidden in the life, is unconfessed, and perhaps unrenounced.

The result is that God will not go up to the battle with the man. The sermon is preached, the prayer uttered, the testimony and exhortation given, considerable intellectual ability displayed, an appearance of something being done is created; and yet devout hearts feel that something is lacking, and victory, clear, glorious, unmistakable victory, does not come. An accursed thing is in the camp; the offender has his tent pitched over it, and the face which looks out of the tent is one of darkness and profound melancholy.

But this is not the explanation of all cases of defeat, nor indeed of the great majority of instances of failure. The blessed power of prevailing with man and obtaining gracious victories in the work of God can be lost in ways far less gross and criminal. It can go through actions which are not the breaking of the letter of the Ten Commandments.

Loose thinking can do the deed.

Careless speech can sap the holy power.

Lack of prayer will affect the divine glow and glory.

Still more remarkable: an undue attention given to things that are lawful and proper in themselves

THE DEFEAT AT AI.

will, in time, leave us weak in the presence of friends and foes.

He who possesses the wonderful blessing which Christ promised the disciples, is called upon to walk in a very narrow way. There are many things which others can do that he can not. He is a Nazarite. There are pursuits which are perfectly honorable, but he can not walk in them. There are books which are untainted, and yet he can not read them. There are songs that are clean, but he can not sing them without hurt to his soul. He may be in the possession of gifts which, if used, might lead him to prominence and wealth. Other men, good and true, tread these paths and are succeeding with gifts not superior to his own; but he is called by the Master to a close walk and a peculiar work. He can not do as others may do.

So, if betrayed by his gifts into these walks and pursuits, he after a while discovers in some important hour that the old-time force has gone. He can not take Ai. It is while he feels his inability to take Ai that he tells how he once captured Jericho. This, of course, is intended as an apology for the present failure, and also helps to while away the time.

The things mentioned may seem too little and insignificant to some to cause such a disaster; but they are not little. A spider-web once took so much electricity from a telegraph wire and buried it in the ground that a message could not be sent from one town to another. The stock company and the public were as much troubled and annoyed about it as if the little white threads were chains of iron. The connection was broken and the power shut off.

There is nothing wrong in the bicycle as used for exercise, health, and business, but the writer knew a holiness preacher who allowed his wheel to so monopolize his thoughts and conversation, and consume so much time in oiling and repairing, that he lost his power and found himself helpless before Ai.

We knew another to devote so much of the day to telegraphy, that should have been spent in communion with God and in soul-work, that the bubbling joy went out of his heart, the shine from his face, and in sermon and prayer you could see that he could not capture Ai.

The writer once had with him for a week or so, while in his active work, a large, sweet-toned music-box. It was only a few days when, through the pathetic sentimental pieces, he felt that a spider-web was getting on his wire. Of course, the box went, for he was anxious to get some messages through to the throne about Ai, which at the same time was holding out most remarkably.

Recently we met a young man who has lost his spiritual joy and power by over-devotion to a musical accomplishment.

A kodak is a pleasant article to possess, and is capable of giving much genuine and innocent pleasure; but if a man, filled with the Holy Ghost and called to a special work, begins to use one too much, he will soon commence wondering where the dew is that was once on the fleece, and what can be the matter with the walls of Ai, which will not go down under his sermons and prayer-guns.

Politics, election returns, Associated Press dispatches, questions of reform, and many other matters can and will, if we are not careful, become switch-lines to take the Divine electricity out of our souls.

Abundance of talk on any ephemeral, non-essential, and temporal question will be a spider-web to the line.

Bicycles, kodaks, telegraphy, music, literature, and art are all good things. They are legitimate and proper, but through them it is possible to lose the old-time glory and power, and we be left everlasting besiegers of Ai, when we should take it at once with a charge and shout of victory.

If we are having continued reverses, meeting with frequent defeats in our religious work and life, let us look under the tent. Small things may be hidden there, and, according to the Bible, God notices small things.

If anything is there to which, while lawful, we give undue attention and devotion, let us correct matters and put them in proper relation.

If anything is there that is doubtful and questionable, we had better dig it up at once and say good-bye to it forever.

If there is a sin, may we not only dig it up, but stone it to death in the valley of Achor. God will then go up with us to the battle; Ai will fall; greater cities still go down, and the inhabitants of the land will tremble at our presence.

XIII.

THE SIFTER AND FAN.

THERE is a great difference between a sifter and fan. They do directly opposite things. The Bible states that the former is used by the devil and the latter by Christ. There is never an interchange or exchange. The character of both forbid it, and the work both are doing would not allow it.

The sifter, as we all will recollect as children, was filled by the cook with meal and then treated to a rapid handshaking. The result of this was that the meal escaped, and only bran was left. This last article, we recall, was thrown out of the kitchen-window on the ground for the chickens to peck at.

In like manner Satan takes a man or woman and sifts them. The idea is to get all the good out of the individual and leave only the bad; to shake out the meal and leave the bran. It is a sickening sight to see a man undergoing this manipulation of the devil's sieve, and behold health, virtue, truth, honor, purity, and every other good thing gradually departing, until at last nothing but the bran of a wasted life, blighted reputation, and undone character is left. We have seen people who had been so thoroughly sifted by Satan, so brought down to bran alone, that it looked like nothing remained for the adversary to do but to knock what was left out of the kitchen-window of hell into the pit for devils to scratch and peck at.

The devil's sieve is a fearful thing. Christ said that the great adversary endeavored to ruin Peter that way. "Simon, Satan hath desired thee that he might sift thee as wheat; but I have prayed for thee that thy faith fail not." In the short time that the enemy was allowed to handle Peter, he had some terrible victories over him, and brought him to the brink of ruin. There are others who do not escape as did the apostle, but are finally and forever undone.

The winnowing fan which Christ is represented as using does the direct opposite of the sifter. A pile of wheat, mixed with chaff, is laid on the floor, and the fan is turned upon it with its strong air current. The result is that the chaff is blown away, and the golden, solid wheat remains. The sifter got rid of the meal and kept the bran; the fan gets rid of the chaff and retains the wheat.

This is Christ's plan and blessed loving work on the souls which belong to him. His omniscient eye sees that in the wheat of devoted religious character there can be downright chaff. And he sees this among the sanctified as well as the regenerated.

We do not mean by chaff that actual or inbred sin

is left, but things that are not best or wise, things that can be removed or improved. Habits, customs, notions, mannerisms, odd ways in particular and general, and certain performances taken up, practiced and exacted of others, that are above the Word, beyond the Word, and not in the Word.

It would require a much larger article than this to mention and describe the various chaffy things that can become mixed up in the wheat of the Christian life, and that should come out, and that from many honest, Christ-like souls is coming out.

One thing is certain,—that we can not pick this chaff out of each other. It would be an endless job, and one that would be resented anyhow. Meanwhile we would be removing the trashy stuff from the life of our brother, he would be doing the same office for us, and there might be a misunderstanding. According to the Bible, it takes Christ to do this work. He blows it out with His winnowing fan. He wants all wheat in His followers and not a particle of chaff. How we ought to love Him for this, and bless God for the steady divine breath that is to blow out of our lives every unwise, foolish, and questionable thing. I repeat that we can have a sanctified heart, and yet can be improved in manners, habits, notions, and many other particulars. Against these things Christ, who has already, with His holy fire, burned up inbred sin, now directs the great winnowing fan of His grace, and they go! Thank God, all of us have both seen and felt some of them go!

I know a brother who was genuinely sanctified, who tried to drive people by abuse into the blessing of perfect love. The Lord turned His fan upon him, and blew the cudgel out of his hands, and he now tries to persuade men into the higher experience. We all recognize among God's people a disposition to exaggerate, especially in description of Church work and revivals. Every meeting is described as a "tornado," a "cyclone" or a "flood." The town is said to be "moved as never before," to be "shaken from center to circumference," and "turned upside down," etc., etc. The actual figures of conquest are not given. Perhaps they would not exactly agree with the other statements about cyclones and tornadoes. The feeling left in the mind after such a letter is that the whole work has been done, and nothing else is left for any one else to do. The writer, in common with many others, has erred on these lines, it being so easy and natural to think, when our own hearts are on fire, and a lot of holiness people are shouting around us, that the whole country is surrendering to God.

A few months ago we read a letter in one of our Church papers from a young preacher, in which he stated that the whole southern part of the State was aroused about a certain Holiness College, and great numbers of young men were coming, etc., etc. The southern part of the State had a population of a million, with a large number of towns. The young man we speak of had been to two or three small communities, and yet wrote as he did. The college register thus far has failed to record the arrival of the southern part of that State.

Against all exaggerated language Christ directs His winnowing fan with the words, "Let your conversation be yea, yea, nay, nay; for whatsoever is more than this cometh of evil."

Again, we know of several godly people who have a way of breaking in upon another person who has been called upon to pray in public, and of keeping up such a verbal clamor that the one who was asked to lead in prayer can not be heard at all. We once held a meeting where not a single prayer was heard for days on account of this strange interruption. As for responses to prayer and ejaculations of praise and joy coming from those around who are listening, we all like and rejoice in. But this was a loud-voiced, verbal drowning out of every prayer offered in the church, except that of this honestly mistaken brother.

The winnowing fan needs to be turned on this unwise habit, while the apostle writes, "Let all things be done in order."

Still again, I meet a religious body of people all over the land that in prayer and exhortation have adopted a whine. As a peculiar nasal utterance it belongs to this denomination. I have never heard any one else adopt it or try to make it their own. Once heard, it can never be forgotten. The people themselves are excellent, and have the solid wheat of a good religious experience, but have mixed up with it this chaff of human addition. God has given us our natural voices, and why we should renounce them, so to speak, in worship, and get to whining the instant we come into His presence and commence praying to Him, I utterly fail to see. The winnowing fan is certainly needed here; not to remove inbred sin, for this has been burned out by the baptism with the Holy Ghost and fire, but to blow away a needless, senseless, and hurtful custom.

The writer knows a number of God's sanctified children who have placed themselves before this fan of Christ, and said, Take out of me and my life, O Lord, everything that is not best and wise. I want to be like you in all things.

It is certainly blessed to see the winnowing-process going on, and to behold these men and women becoming more spiritually lovely and attractive all the time. They get so loving, gentle, patient, discreet, level-headed, restful, and Christ-like that we rejoice to meet and be with them. We find ourselves wishing that all of God's people were like them; fierceness, combativeness, argumentativeness, offensive peculiarities and mannerisms, unscriptural notions and practices all given up, the chaff gone, and the beautiful, golden wheat of a modest, humble, faithful Christian life and character left for hell to be amazed at, earth to admire, and heaven to rejoice over.

May the good Lord turn His winnowing fan upon us all! If we are all wheat, we have nothing to dread or lose. If we have chaff, it ought to go. We wonder how many will say Amen.

XIV.

"THE BATTLE IS NOT YOURS."

THIS was God's message to His people when the enemy, in overwhelming numbers, were arrayed against them. It is a message that needs to be sent and received to-day fully as much as upon that morning, when the forces encamped against Israel were like grasshoppers for multitude.

The sentence of five words, which forms the caption of this article, is susceptible of two applications. First, it may come in rebuke. There are some people who act as if the whole Church rested upon their shoulders. These characters are found both in the ministry and laity. They go about with pondering brows, anxious looks, and burdened spirits. The care of the Church or Churches proves a crushing load to them. To some they appear to be the door of the Church, to others they seem to have the keys, and to still others they look like they not only run the visible kingdom of Christ, but actually bear it up. To the young and uninitiated these personages, with their burdened, even oppressed, appearance, are very awe-inspiring.

The writer recalls a certain large building in one

of our great cities, which has near its foundation a row of Satyr-like figures. They are bowed down as if they were upholding the vast fabric above, when the truth is, as the architect will tell you, they have only the appearance of supporting, and really bear up nothing. A number of times we have seen individuals in the Church, who reminded us of these stone images. They carry a burdened look, a strained expression of countenance, as if they could not hold out much longer. They bear themselves as if, through the neglect and faithlessness of others, great and crushing burdens had been laid upon them, when the truth was that the financial and religious welfare of the Church did not depend upon them at all. We have all seen this character in the home, business-office, and many other places; but for richness of expression, completeness of outline, as well as fullness of detail, we have to go to the Church to behold the man. He may be a presiding elder, pastor, steward, or Church member, it does not matter; the facial expression born of the imagination that a fearful responsibility is upon him, and one out of all proportion greater than that which rests upon the other members of the Church, is unmistakably there. In addition can be read in the mystic handwriting on the countenance the inward belief that he is the only one of the Lord's prophets now left in the land, and that if he should die—well, there is no language powerful enough to describe the extent of the woe which would befall the Church at the loss of such a servant, who, not content with being a pillar, actually bears up the pillars themselves! In a word, he has unwittingly made himself the foundation.

So they all have a "bearing-up" look. An awful load, not only of personal but of general responsibility, seems to be crushing them to the earth. They try to cultivate a meek silence at times, but it will not and does not last; they must speak and recount what they have done, are doing, and are going to do; the last being always the greatest of the three. In one case I recall a steward who, on one of his monthly laudations of what he had done and suffered for Zion, ran out of facts concerning actual performances, and said, "Brethren, I can't even sleep at night for thinking of these things." The "these things" to which he referred was a debt of several hundred dollars on a Church which never paid less than fifteen thousand dollars a year for all purposes, and never had a deficit to report at the Annual Conference. The brother knew this, but he must have some grievance in order to be able to give a reason for the grief which was in him. The sadly amusing feature of it all was that he was a well-to-do man, and could easily have paid the bill, and not missed the money. But he wanted to "grieve" instead of "give." Two small letters make a great difference in words.

The grief-stricken appearance I have beheld in some Church officials, and the sighs I have heard them heave, would give them fame in the world of drama, and command any price as "wailers" and "mourners" for funerals in the far-away East.

Time was in my early ministry when I was much impressed with this class of people, and thought everything rested upon them, that nothing would or could be more calamitous than the death of these same nervous, wiry, jerky, fussy, busy, consequential individuals.

Little by little I began to see that the Church did not rest upon them; that others, who were saying but little, were really doing more, and much more, than these same persons, and not only financially, but in every other way, for the cause of Christ.

Then, I have seen one of these deluded beings die; and it was simply marvelous to note how well God's cause got along without him; in fact, that an actual sense of relief was realized. Only think of it! Not a jar was felt through all the vast and complicated machinery of the Church; not a halt of a single moment upon the part of God's mighty advancing hosts. Multiplied thousands were being saved while he was dying. Hundreds of millions never heard of him, and, awful to state, among the few who knew him, no one was inconsolable at his departure. And yet he imagined that he was not only important, but essential.

The expression, "We can not get along without him," even when uttered in connection with the best and most useful of men, is not only untrue, but perfectly absurd.

The Orientals had a figurative way of conveying truth, which was very powerful. One of their symbolic sermons was to thrust a finger into water, and then, upon withdrawing it, ask the looker-on to show them the hole. The lesson was, that just that much we would be missed on the earth; that, the instant we were withdrawn from the walks of life, men would rush in instantly, and so fill our places; we would never be missed.

Let the reader ask himself what physician, lawyer, merchant, or preacher has arrested by his death the onward sweep of his profession or calling.

But the people of whom we speak will not be so taught and convinced. They are settled in the idea that they, like Atlas, bear up everything. So they go on in their delusion, while their brethren also go on, but smiling as they go, at this conceit, which, if it were true, would wreck the Church with the death of every such man.

But the expression, "The battle is not yours," is also one of comfort.

If the battle is not ours, then it is the Lord's. Here at once we get the consolation, and see the victory. If God's people would only allow this fact to take possession of mind and heart, what an amount of fret and anxiety they would be delivered from! In the great moral struggle going on around the world, God is leading. It is His war. While He uses us, it is His power, truth, and presence which is to win the day at last.

All of God's children who have in them a proper concern for the welfare and spread of His kingdom in the world have several blessed facts for their consolation.

One is, that God took care of the Church quite a while before they were born. He brought the truth up out of the Dark Ages when the Devil seemed to have the world in an everlasting grasp. If the Lord did this when Bibles were scarce and faithful men few, what reason for hope and joy have we now, with the broad flashlight of the gospel flung in every direction, with countless copies of the Scriptures, and a vast body of consecrated and sanctified men and women altogether given up to the Lord!

Another fact is, that the gospel will **continue to**

roll on its victorious way after we are dead. Elijah has to go, but God is getting Elisha ready to take his place. George Fox is called away, but John Wesley takes up the same cry which died away on the Quaker's whitening lips. The Methodist Church began to lose power, and the Salvation Army sprang to the front after sinners. A cold, stiff ecclesiasticism creeps like death toward the heart of the Church, and God sweeps the holiness movement around the world. So it goes. You need not be afraid to die, my brother; draw up your feet, turn your face to the wall, and be gathered to your fathers. The Church will manage to get along after you are gathered. The gospel-car, loaded down with happy passengers, will be rushing through the land, while you, poor, dear heart, will be gasping for breath. The old ship of Zion will be coming up the stream of Time, the banks resounding with the shouts of the redeemed, while you are being lowered in the grave.

If a dead Christian could look out of the glass case of his coffin, or take a peep out of the grave on Sunday morning after his burial, he would be surprised to see how many had taken his place and were rushing on with the banner of salvation.

It was a custom in Greece, when tidings of an important nature were sent, for it to be borne by a man with a flaming firebrand. As he sank exhausted, another man caught it up ere it fell, and so on, until at last the flambeau, with its figurative message, had reached the point of destination. So runs and falls the gospel messenger, and so others quickly take up the good news, the tidings of great joy to all people, and have borne it far away while the dying Christian is breathing his last, surrounded by friends and family.

A third consolation is the thought that, as the battle is the Lord's, he is bound to win.

Viewed in any light, there can be no question about the matter. How can one who is omnipresent, omniscient, and omnipotent, be overcome? If the Lord was afraid of the issue, He could easily stop the generation of the human family until we all died out; or he could remove the oxygen from the air, or send a flood, or make the earth open, and swallow us up out of sight, or with a blow of His almighty hand shiver the earth to pieces, and let us fall forever through the bottomless space which underlies the universe.

But God sees fit not to defeat us by physical might, but with moral and spiritual forces. It makes the battle longer, but the victory not the less certain. So wonderful is His power that He overrules everything, makes the wrath of man to praise Him, and declares that all things shall work together for good to us if we but love Him.

More than all that, the very end of the war has been foreseen and described by Heaven. It is overwhelming victory for God and His people, and eternal disaster and irrevocable defeat to Satan and his followers. The very language of sinners in their fear and despair at the Last Day has been given, when they ask for mountains and rocks to fall on them, and hide them from the face of Him who sits upon the throne. A picture, taken of the closing scene, shows the Devil with the false prophet in hell, with all the nations that forget God; while Jesus reigns from sun to sun, holiness is everywhere, and the New Jerusalem is seen descending from the skies.

Surely, in view of all these things, the child of God should be no pessimist, but look up, and be glad, for God is with us, and the day of earth's redemption draweth nigh.

XV.

THE TEST OF SUCCESS AND FAILURE.

A MORAL test is not necessarily a temptation. The Devil tempts, while God tests His people. In those days, the Bible says, God did tempt Abraham. The commentators tell us, the better reading is that God tried or tested Abraham. The Scripture is clear in the statement that God tempts no man. Moreover, our knowledge of Him precludes the idea.

But God can place us in certain circumstances and situations, can pass us through various conditions of life, which will reveal and declare who we are and where we are in the spiritual life. These testings come to all. They vary somewhat, yet are similar with many. They appear with remarkable vividness in Elijah's life, and as we study them, they seem reflections or pictures of our own.

In Elijah's case we notice the test of success.

The prophet had won a great victory on Mount Carmel. The fire had fallen, he had been vindicated and honored by God, the people were convinced, and the prophets of Baal had been slain by hundreds. Through all this amazing success he kept in his proper place before God, was humble and true as ever, and went from this triumph to another on the brow of the mountain, where he pleaded with the Lord, and received rain for the parched country. He stood the test of success.

Not all can stand it. Many have gone down under it, and many more will yet do so. Some Christians lose their heads immediately upon a first clearly-marked success. Others run well for a while, and then, as victory after victory comes to them on different lines of the Christian life, they begin to falter, totter, and then topple from their high attainments and close walk with God.

They went up the ladder of temporal promotion too rapidly. The elevation was so sudden, and the position so lofty, as to create dizziness. Frequent success in the work of the Lord brought about public praise, newspaper notices, various kinds of compliments, which at last sapped the strength, stole away the humility, and destroyed the power of one of God's devoted servants.

The harm was not all done at once, but spiritual people could see the damage being inflicted, and beheld it with intense sorrow. The man, once so humble, developed spiritual pride before he was aware of it. He can not endure contradiction. He finds it difficult to pardon a criticism passed on himself or work. He has a keen relish for praise; it is like incense in his nostrils. He does not care to hear others complimented; it is wearisome to him. He wants the censer swung before him mainly, if not altogether; and if it is not done, he drops hints to bring about the swinging of the sweet thing. Time was that newspaper puffs and notices humbled him, but now he carefully cuts them out or sends marked copies of the paper to individuals or to others papers, that the echo of his greatness might dwell long in the land.

He is a spiritually fallen man. He has an idol in his life, and it is himself. He is a self-worshipper. He says that it is not so, but it is evident to all that Christ has really the second place in his life. He was once great in his littleness, but is now little in his greatness. The trouble is that he does not realize it. God knows it, men see it, but he, the fallen one, is the last to recognize it. God, in His goodness, will yet show His servant these melancholy things. The pillow of the Satan-deceived and fame-deluded man will yet be wet with bitter tears over the fact that he could not stand success; that he was faithful enough in a humble and obscure sphere, but lost his head completely when elevation and promotion came.

Few men can stand success. All are willing to risk it, and thousands who enter upon that condition get spiritually hurt, and, worse still, go into backsliding, and some into gross sin.

We recently heard some grave-eyed, serious-faced men speaking of Hobson, the hero of the Merrimac. They were deploring his late conduct and the remarkable weakness he was exhibiting. One of them said, "He could not stand success; the flattery of a nation was too great for him." The silence which followed the remark was eloquent as well as pathetic; all felt the words of the speaker were true.

We never hear a young preacher much praised, but we tremble for him. No one can tell the harm that has been done here by indiscreet Christian men and women. It is true that the flattered, patted, and petted man of God says that he needs all this kind of word-incense and tongue-anointings; but a glance at the spiritual giants of the Bible—Joseph, Elijah, Daniel, and Paul—shows that they had none of this coddling and nursing, taffying and sugar-plumming.

Few can stand it. Few can be trusted on pinnacles. Few can wield the scepter of any kind of power without making a bludgeon of it to others and finally a tripping-stick for himself. Under the strange, intoxicating influence of public notice, public applause, and the dizziness of high position,—behold, the simplicity and sincerity of Christ is lost. The humble man grows haughty, the once lowly child of God becomes domineering, and the meek, obscure preacher in time evolves into a dreaded ecclesiastical tyrant and autocrat.

A friend of the writer saw a man elected to the highest position in the Church. He said that in twelve hours the "swelling" of the man was painfully apparent to his best friends.

Few can stand success and power. Some, thank God, like Elijah, can do so; may their tribe increase! But many can not; down they go. Look at them tottering already! See them falling! Hear the crash! My God, have mercy!

A second moral test is that of failure.

This is the opposite of the other. It is to see the work of our hands fail, or apparently fail. It may be a failure of a single effort, a series of efforts, or a lifetime work.

In Elijah's case it was the apparent defeat of the greatest purpose and effort of his life. He was looking for a result that would honor God and bless the people. His victory on Mount Carmel, his triumph in prayer on the brow of the mountain overlooking the sea, and the destruction of Baal's prophets, had prepared him to expect the complete overthrow of idolatry in Israel and the universally-accepted and peaceably-restored worship of God. To his amazement this does not follow, but instead he gets a message from Queen Jezebel that she is determined to have his life, and that speedily. The Scripture tells us that when Elijah heard that, "He went for his life." Then followed his dejection under the juniper-tree and his low spirits in the cave on the mountain. In his own words,—"he wanted to die." He who stood the test of success and glorious victory went down under the test of temporary reverse or apparent failure.

As a rule, a less number lose spiritual ground here than through the test of success. Still many weaken and go down at this point, so that the lesson is needed to be taught and the warning-signal held up.

With failure comes the falling away of friends. It is sad to say, and can be said without bitterness or cynicism, that there is a class of admirers and followers who are simply fair-weather adherents. They can go from Bethany to Jerusalem with an acclaiming crowd with you, but fall away in the journey from the Judgment Hall to Calvary. They are enraptured with one's success, but when the tide of popularity or prosperity seems to turn, they also turn.

One does not have to live long to see this most melancholy feature of human nature. If ever a man needed comfort and sympathy, it is when adversity comes, when a strange revolution of life's wheel pulls him down in temporal things, and heavy hands of power and influence are outstretched to keep him down. Now is the time for the grasp of the hand, the cheery smile, the warm word of love, the sympathetic visit, or the reassuring letter. But not always do these things come, and, worse still, from where they might have been expected.

This forsaking, turning away, and cooling off towards one in misfortune, has been seen even in the home. Men in fine financial condition have had a court and deference paid them by their families, which they imagined to be the outcroppings of love and devotion; but when trouble came, and they could not do as formerly, they discovered a failure in attention and an absence of affection, which first surprised and grieved, and then, as the cause flashed upon the mind, shocked and hardened them.

Here comes in, then, the power of failure. It alters our surroundings, seems to change people, shakes one's confidence in those formerly trusted, and so opens the heart wide to sorrow, despair, and a profound spirit of skepticism as to many things and all people.

An additional feature of failure is a certain loneliness attendant upon it. The successful man is sought after, the failing man is let alone. Elijah had the entire wilderness to himself after his rebuff and defeat at Jezreel. In like manner men are allowed to have solitary hours, lonely days, and empty rooms after failure comes.

Let a man fail in a speech or sermon, and he will be struck with the fact, how few will hunt him up. It is the man who carried everything before him, and who needs no human comfort, who is surrounded and fairly covered up with congratulations.

Let a man lose his fortune, or his business position, or fail in a great undertaking, or come short of what was expected of him by his friends, and at once he hears the sighing of the wilderness around him, and knows that in heart and life he is alone.

This is a crucial hour, a most wonderful opportunity in the character-world, a battle-field for either a great victory or equally stupendous defeat. What shall it be? Will the man rise or sink? Will he push on or stop? Will he rise superior to the test or go down under it?

While it is the soul's glorious opportunity, it is also Satan's hour. Here he has captured great numbers, as, lying under the juniper-tree, they said they were no better than their fathers, that hope was in vain, and they only craved for themselves the privilege to die.

Happy the man who will stand the test, push

on through the desert, hold to his faith in God, and keep the sweetness and cleanness of his soul in spite of everything. He shall come into the "confirmed," "strengthened," "established," "settled" experience which Paul writes about, and after that obtain the crown of glory that fadeth not away.

XVI.

THE TEST OF WANT AND RELIEF.

ALL the sides of a man's character are not touched by the tests of success and failure. There is a mighty trying force in loneliness, and an equally powerful one in being thrown constantly for days or months or years with what is called the crowd or multitude. Each peculiar condition will reveal some weakness of the heart, and call for attention and upbuilding at a place where feebleness was not suspected.

After a while may come the test of want.

This means not simply the loss of many comforts, but positive need itself. This trial came to Elijah far from infrequently. Driven by persecution to deserts and caves, comforts, doubtless, he never knew, while oftentimes a bare subsistence was his lot. And there were times when his need was so great that it required a miracle from heaven to keep him from starvation.

Elijah was the most faithful servant God had in Judah or Israel, and yet there was no one who seemed to have a harder time in what is called the temporalities of life. At the time we now write of, he was dwelling in a cave far away from towns and cities, and was fed by ravens, and drank at the brook which flowed in front of the cavern. He seemed to have had but two meals a day, and the fare was not sumptuous. Of course, Satan was busy at this point, to call the prophet's attention to the comfortable, not to say luxurious, living of the prophets of Baal, of the three hundred whom Queen Jezebel had fed at her own table, while he, God's servant, living the truth, and preaching the truth, spent most of his life in exile, suffering, and actual want.

One day he noticed that the brook which murmured before his hiding-place, did not flow with as great volume as on the preceding day. The following day it had still diminished, and Elijah saw it steadily lessen, its tinkle weaken, until it became a mere thread of water, a trickle, and then finally a dry bed of sand and rock.

There is not the slightest intimation in the Book that the prophet's faith failed in this trying circumstance or that he became impatient or repining. That the opportunity was golden for such a mental and spiritual state, none can question. But the man of God stood true to God and himself through it all.

Not all, however, can claim such a victory. It is a bitter trial to be needy, even when we have brought poverty on ourselves by indolence or a sinful, spendthrift life. But there is a keener pang sometimes in the thought that our stripping and need comes while walking in the ways of righteousness. The great enemy is quick to call attention to the fact. The soul is requested to note the prosperity of the wicked, that they have all that heart can wish, and spread themselves like a green bay-tree, while the child of God has the dust thrown upon him by their flying carriage-wheels, and in many cases can not see twenty-four hours ahead, so far as daily bread is concerned.

It constitutes an experience never to be forgotten to see the brook of one's income steadily diminishing and drying up, to hear the tinkle of temporal prosperity getting fainter with the flight of each day,—more than that, to behold the gaunt form of Need leaning against the door, looking in, and, later on, walking in, and taking his place in the house as one of the family, his presence after that being as constantly realized as that of any member of the household.

Bishop Marvin tells of the profound impression made upon him as a child, by his father and mother looking together, one day, into their almost emptied corn-crib, and talking gloomily about the future. He said, their anxious faces and low voices rolled a burden even on his boyish heart, and made a solemn memory that time had never been able to obliterate.

When a Christian, steady, straightforward, and true, spends his life in an everlasting financial strain and pinch, and sees at the same time men of the world with their comfortable homes and easy incomes, and whose lives are not such as they should be, he is going through a test.

When a preacher, with an inadequate salary, one on which he finds it impossible to do justice to his children in the way of education and preparation for life, looks across the street, and sees a lawyer, whose beautiful home and grounds declare not only comfort, but luxury; when he contrasts these happenings in his mind with the added thought that he is doing far more good in the world than the lawyer, the man is passing through a test, and a severe one at that.

When an evangelist goes to a place, and labors with all his mind, soul, and strength for the spiritual good of the community, and sees scores of souls saved and blessed under his ministry, and receives far less for the ten days' work than some strolling lecturer with a "funny subject" obtains in a single night's address, there is a fine opportunity here for repining, not to say discouragement. When this same evangelist, after one month's hard gospel labor, had scarcely an amount above traveling expenses given him for compensation, and landed at his home on Christmas eve with two dollars in his pocket, a very great spiritual test was brought to bear upon such **qualities as patience, faith, and loyalty to a divine work.**

A letter, received from a devout young Christian woman, contained such a portrayal of absolute want in the large family of which she was a member, of the brook having completely dried up, that the heart literally ached as we read the lines.

Of course, these conditions throw the life open to violent and persistent assaults of the Devil, the temptations being in the direction of unbelief, bitterness, worldly pursuits, compromise of principle and character, and other lines too numerous to mention.

The child of God who can see the brook diminish, and then disappear, whose bread comes by weight, and day by day, and as by a miracle, and yet keep sweet, patient, believing, and faithful in the Savior's work all the time, has about graduated in one of the highest schools in the spiritual life. He has swept up out of the class of "The Thirty," and is one of the famous "Three" spoken of in the Old Testament.

The opposite test of want is that of relief.

The idea we would present is, that the mode which God often adopts to deliver the Christian in his troubles is often as faith-trying as the condition of need in which he was plunged.

This thought is brought out by considering the manner in which God relieved his servant Elijah. It was a time of famine in the land, and yet the Lord did not send the prophet to a wealthy man to be taken care of, but to a poor widow, and she so poverty-stricken that she had only a handful of meal left in her barrel. Again Elijah rose victorious over the new test, and, believing it was all right, told the woman to make the cake of bread out of that last meal, and doubt nothing. His mighty faith stimulated and invigorated her sinking heart, and she did so. It was a wonderful biscuit that she made that day. It proved to be perfectly abundant for the needs of three people, not only all that day, but as long as the famine lasted.

The reader can not but recall occasions of distress, financial, spiritual, and other kinds, where relief came in ways and methods that were utterly unexpected. The time, manner, and instrument are scarcely ever what the tried one looked for, and in that fact we behold God even in the hour of deliverance quickening and developing faith in the soul. Man in his wisdom would not have conceived of succor in that way; reason would not have planned it in such a fashion. The deliverance of God, like all His other tests, is to intensify and strengthen faith. God is pledged to relieve his child, but the method and time is of Divine selection, and with every repetition is bound to strengthen the man's confidence in the love and faithfulness of the Almighty. Besides, the waiting itself develops faith. Who would have dreamed that the Lord would have commanded the poorest woman in the country to take care of His servant? But He did so, and the method of relief was an overwhelming argument and proof of God's ability to provide for His people in the most discouraging circumstances, and so an inspiration to faith and perfect soul-restfulness. How could a man doubt after such an unmistakably providential dealing?

A Christian woman, brought to sore straits, and almost yielding to despair, had to be comforted, and faith in God renewed. The agency the Lord used to revive and restore His child was the sight of a sparrow hopping about on the snow-covered ground. Instantly the words of Christ rushed over her, "Your heavenly Father feedeth them—are ye not much better than they?" The revulsion of feeling was complete as, with ascendant faith in her heart, and happy tears in her eyes, she murmured, "If He cares for sparrows, how much more will He care for me!"

One of the most gifted preachers in the South, Dr. C. K. Marshall, had suddenly lost two beautiful children. He and his wife were prostrated under the blow. In the very blackest day of their sorrow they were, one morning, in their bedroom, too stunned and heartsick to take up the simplest duty. How, now, shall they be helped? Who is qualified to talk to and help this prince of pulpit orators, who knew beforehand all that any one could say to him?

The strangeness of God's methods of relief is again seen in the way He remembered His gifted servant. Prominent, learned, and cultivated people had come and gone, with their conversations, prayers, expressions of sympathy, and counsel. All had failed. One day God sent a poor old colored washerwoman, who, standing at the foot of the bed, and looking down with streaming eyes and kindling face upon the prostrate man and his wife by his side, so held up the duty of submission to God, the certainty of reunion in heaven, and, above all, the fact of an ever-present, loving, sympathetic Christ, that the fountains of the deep were broken up in the souls of the two she addressed, the stony feeling was swept away, a tide of sweetest spiritual consolation filled their hearts, and life, with its burdens and duties, was taken up from that hour with a comfort and power never before realized. The instrument of relief was a negro woman, poor, unlettered, and unknown to the world, but well known to God and filled with the Holy Ghost.

We heard a gentleman say in Alabama, a couple of years ago, that he became convicted for his sins at a meeting, and there came a night when he was so burdened that he thought he would go wild with grief and despair. The services were over, the meeting had ended, all in the household were asleep, and he tossed, wakeful and miserable, upon his bed. By his side, sound asleep, was a tobacco-chewing, backslidden preacher. There was no need of waking him up, for he himself was spiritually lapsed and dead. While thus situated, who but God could give relief? It was a summer night, the windows were open, and the katydids were singing by scores in the trees. Suddenly God made the choral chirp or song sound exactly like "Come to Jesus," "Come to Jesus." With a burst of tears the man cried out, "I will," fell upon his knees by the bedside, and was instantly saved.

In the first year of his ministry, the writer, like many other preachers, had a very hard time financially. He saw the brook get smaller every day, and finally, after living on bread alone for several days, saw even that give out. The weather, also, was bitter cold, and his coal supply was exhausted. As the town in which he lived was not on his circuit, there was no one to look to or call on. He had well-to-do men on his work, but they, in the rush of their own life and business, had overlooked him. What would God do in this case?

At four o'clock in the afternoon the young preacher, with a perfectly empty storeroom in his house, knelt down before his stove, and cast in the last lump of coal he had. Without rising, he dropped his face in his hands, and said, with tears in his voice as well as eyes, "Lord, I will trust you," when suddenly there was a knock at the front door of the cottage home, and on the doorstep stood a poor farmer's boy. He said, with a kind voice, but in a bashful way, to the preacher:

"I have just sold the bale of cotton I made this year, and have brought you four dollars. I have heard you preach several times, and want to help you."

Doubtless the young man wondered, as he turned away, why the preacher's voice was so broken as he thanked him, and why tears should fall over such a small present. But it was not small in the sight of God or of the man benefitted. Moreover, the preacher saw back of the brown hand of the country-boy the white hand of Christ. He was at His old work of breaking bread. Then was the Scripture verified, "And the word of the Lord came unto Elijah, saying, Arise, get thee to Zarephath, and dwell there; behold, I have commanded a widow woman there to sustain thee."

May the Lord grant us to be as faithful under the two tests of want and relief as was His servant Elijah! And for our additional strength and comfort may we not forget that Christ was brought into want, and had the Devil to whisper to Him in the wilderness, "Why can not these stones be turned into bread?" He stood the test to the end, even forty days; and then came the relief. It was wonderful. The Bible says that "Angels came and ministered unto him." The same will be done to us if we abide in Christ and remain faithful.

XVII.

THE WITHERED HAND.

THE hand is king among the members. It is hardly possible to overrate its value to the body. If the eyes fail, the hand becomes, through touch, a second sight; if the tongue is dumb, the hand, through signs and gesticulation, furnishes not only words, but a language itself. Oratory without the hand is almost like a bird without wings, while the great body of musical instruments, thus deprived, become nothing but pieces of furniture.

But there are other offices of the hand, which, when we apply to the spiritual life, will add a painful interest to the spectacle presented by the Gospel in the words that, in the congregation listening to Christ, there was a man whose hand was withered. This meant much, when viewed alone in a physical sense, but with a spiritual application, a far greater trouble and calamity is prevented.

There are many withered hands in Christian congregations and assemblies to-day. As the lame man lay at the Beautiful Gate, and the palsied man was stretched by the Pool of Bethesda, so these withered ones are in the Church, under the wings of the cherubim, and in the immediate presence of the God of grace, love, and power.

There are a thousand blessed and beautiful things these people could do with their hands if they were not withered. Some have never done anything; others were once useful, but have ceased doing. The sinner's hand and the backslider's hand are wonderfully alike in the fact that just now both are lifeless and powerless. One was always so; the other was healed for a season, for a while did great good, and then something happened, known to God and themselves, and now, although still in the house of worship, they are present with a withered hand.

We once knew a lady whose right hand became paralyzed. She carried it on a pillow. It was smooth and plump, but had a dead white look that was corpselike. This useless, lifeless hand was literally loaded with diamonds and emerald rings. We never looked upon the helpless member, covered with sparkling jewels, without a sense of pain, as well as disgust. And it is with no pleasant sensation we look upon the beautiful, well-kept, and even jeweled hands in the Church, and think of the little good they are doing for Christ in this world. Another dead thing is loaded down with gems!

One office of the spiritual hand is, to give the grasp of interest and love.

It would be impossible to estimate the good which has been done by such a clasp. It is a means of grace to both parties. Men and women can date the great moral change of their lives to such a cordial grasp of the hand. Such a pressure given the writer, when he had turned his back on the world, was like a great influx of strength to his soul. And yet this needed work of the hand is lacking in so many places because it is withered.

Another office of the hand is, to uplift the fallen.

There are many hands and weapons lifted to push and knock people down who are treading the way of life. And there are hands to keep them down. And then, thank God, there are hands to lift men up. They are few in comparison with the others, but they exist for all that.

It is always counted a noble act for a man to pluck one from the fire or the waves, or to deliver from any great physical danger. Men commemorate such deeds in marble, in medals, and in song, oration, and book. The land resounds with the achievement in which a hand went down, and a human life came up.

There are greater dangers than fire and flood; and mightier perils than falling buildings and plunging derailed trains; and greater despairs born in the heart than that of feeling a vessel going down in mid-ocean, or beholding the flames cutting off all hope of escape from a burning building. There are such things as hopeless poverty, present crushing want, profound moral mistakes, sins committed, character wrecked, reputation gone, conscience on fire, and devils goading the heart to desperation. Where one sinks in the sea, or is ingulfed in blazing houses, thousands are going down here, and the sad thought is, that they would not have gone down if there had not been so many withered hands in the Church.

We knew a man who had a number of disasters befall him. Finally, one morning, a greater trouble than all, which had gone before, befell him in his business. Stunned, heartsick, despairing, he took the street-cars for home. On the cars he met a friend and member of the Church, who noticed his sorrow, but said nothing. He reached home, and almost staggered into his wife's room, hungry for a look and word and grasp of sympathy and love. The wife was so absorbed in her young baby that she had scarcely a glance for her wretched husband. He told her that he was in great distress, and her cold reply was to go in the next room, and lie down. A hand-clasp of love and pity would have saved him even then, but it did not come. He was married to a woman who had a withered hand when it came to spiritual help. He, with a groan, walked into the next room, and committed suicide.

Few active, devoted workers but have thrilling histories to relate of timely help that, under God, they were able to extend, and that prevented desperate deeds, robbed hell of a victim, and added a new citizen to the kingdom of God. Look on us, said Peter to the lame man, and at the same time gave him his hand, and Luke says, the afflicted one leaped to his feet. Save us from a hand that is idly folded into its fellow-palm, and coddled in its deathlikeness on a pillow, and gemmed when it is doing nothing for God or man worth a copper cent. Give us the hand that can reach downward, and get hold of a despairing heart and sinking life, and lift them up, and present them to God. Such a hand Christ carried with Him, and such a hand we should all pray to possess.

A third office of the hand is, to give.

The sight of a woman stopping on the street to give to a beggar has always warmed my heart. The spectacle of a liberal man giving his gold, silver, and bank-notes to a worthy cause is always an uplifting sight. The human race is united in condemnation and disgust of a miser, and all agree in admiring and praising the generous and princely giver. No statue is built for an avaricious man who hoarded and lived for himself; but the man whose heart-throbs broke the fastenings of his front door, and the latch of his gate, and helped the outside world in its need and distress as God gave him ability,—this is the man whose name is pronounced with love and gratitude, and whose life is honored everywhere. He has built monuments for himself in churches, colleges, and good institutions of various kinds. The tears which he dried by his benefactions to the poor will reappear, transformed into flashing gems, that will deck his crown at the Last Day. The blessings he receives from countless lips will be woven into a marvelous robe of glory for him in the coming world.

. Few know how to give. The hand is withered. The man can not get his fingers into his pocket, and has no strength to draw out his purse, or to extract coins and bills from its folds. Poor, lifeless member that can not respond to the call which comes up from starving people in our alleys for bread and coal, and from the jungles of India and Africa for gospel light and salvation!

A fourth office of the hand is, to supplicate in prayer to God, and bring down the power of Heaven upon the people.

We naturally fold or clasp the hands when we pray, and often they are uplifted in supplication. The more earnest the petition becomes, the more the hand is used. We have all seen such hands. There have been times that we have beheld them over the heads ot a congregation, when they reminded us of banners, leading on to battle and victory. Some of them would get hold of the throne, and would bring down the Spirit upon the audience in mighty power. There were no pillars and galleries lined and loaded with such spiritual difficulty and opposition but they could, by the might of those hands of prayer, bring the whole thing down before God with a perfect crash.

How we bless God for these hands of prayer! We see them in many places, at the sick-bed, dying-bed, family altar, Sunday-school, prayer-meeting, and Church service. They are barricades between souls and ruin, and they, at the same time, are great levers to pry men and women out of sin and despair into hope and righteousness.

It is said of Stonewall Jackson that he could be seen, during the raging of the battle, with his head bowed and right hand uplifted in prayer, as he galloped up and down in front of firing and charging lines. Who wonders at his victories? God would not let anything override that lifted hand. And it has seemed to the writer that, while God intended to emancipate the slave in the Civil War, yet He had to bury that man before He could let the invading army roll on to accomplish the great design. God honors the uplifted hand.

When a certain battle took place between the Israelites and one of their powerful enemies, the Bible says that Moses went up on a mountain, and lifted his hands in prayer. The Scripture adds that, when his hands drooped, Amalek prevailed, but when they were steady in their uplifted position, Israel prevailed. The efficacy of fervent, importuning prayer is plainly taught here in this striking occurrence.

In view of all-this, how exceedingly melancholy it is to see the withered hands in the Church! They are busy in Church festivals, they can clap an elegant approval of some song in a social reception, but they hang pale and lifeless when we enter the realm of prayer and importunate pleadings for salvation, full salvation, and the mighty power of God to come upon the people.

What a time we would have, and how the kingdom of hell would be shaken, if all the hands, now numbered as Christian, could be restored and filled with life and power as we have mentioned, and be lifted triumphantly to the skies! Who doubts, if this were done, Israel would prevail, and sin and Satan would go down everywhere?

Christ's remedy for the withered hand is to stretch it forth. This is what He told the man thus afflicted before him, and he, in the effort to obey, suddenly felt life and strength rush into the dead member.

If the withered hand is that of the unconverted

man, the thing to do is to fix the eyes on Christ, and try to do with the paralyzed soul what He commands to be done.

If the hand has become withered from disuse or sin, and is that of the backslider, then sin is to be renounced, and the long unused powers of the life must be dedicated again to God, and the effort to obey in all things be made, while the eye all the while is steadily fixed on Christ.

The repentance of the backslider, whether he has lapsed in the regenerated or sanctified life, is to do the first works, take up neglected duties, and obey God in every particular. The heart is sick, and the hand is heavy, but He who made us bids the drooping-hearted man to stretch forth the withered hand. Return to forsaken fields of duty, resume the old-time benevolences, go to helping and assisting the needy and fallen, invade the realms of importunate prayer again, give heart, tongue, foot, hand, and voice once more fully to God. In a word, with eyes fixed on Christ, stretch forth the withered hand.

Reason will say, it is hopeless. Feeling may urge you to wait for more emotion. Despair may whisper, nothing will come of it; and the Devil may tempt you not to do so, but Jesus says, stretch it forth. So, in His beloved name, do it! The instant that you do so, healing life, restoration, joy, and blessedness will rush into the spirit, and another being will be seen who has a tongue to praise God, a foot to leap at His bidding, and a hand, withered no longer, but able to lift up the fallen, give freely to the needy, and pull down the blessings of Heaven upon hundreds and thousands of struggling immortal souls.

XVIII.

THE SMITTEN MOUTH.

PAUL had been arrested by ecclesiastical authority, and was standing before the Sanhedrim under the charge of being an enemy to the Church. Being allowed to speak for himself, he said, "Men and brethren, I have lived in all good conscience before God until this day." This was a first-class experience, and one that few can truly claim as their own, and yet it was instantly met with the loud, harsh command of the high priest, "Smite him on the mouth!"

It would seem from this that an experience of a high order was not relished by the scribes and doctors of the temple. Perhaps there is an element of condemnation in the relation of high spiritual attainment or obtainment to religious people who have degenerated into men of Church affairs, whose eyes have been diverted from the Spirit in the wheels to the wheels themselves. The Sanhedrim lived for the machinery, but Paul had seen "a man's hand in the wheels." It had a scar in the palm. To say that he had beheld more than the high priest and the elders, was not only presumptuous, but unpardonable, and called at once for a crushing blow on the lips which had given such umbrage.

It is an old offense and an old punishment. Christ Himself, long before Paul's mishap, had in like manner outraged the same high ecclesiastical circle, and received a similar cruel blow upon His mouth. And yet He had simply declared the truth in every word which He had uttered.

It seems that some men do not want to hear the truth, or anyhow the whole truth. They live obviously on lower planes of the spiritual life, and yet would speak advisedly about the higher planes. Under the plea of attending to the "wheels," to the various Sanhedrim meetings of the Church, they have overlooked the privilege, duty, and necessity of waiting ten days in humble supplication and expectancy before God in the upper room. Giving only a few minutes of each day to God in real prayer on their knees, they feel perfectly competent to sit in judgment upon servants of God who daily pray from three to four hours upon their faces. Living at the foot of the mountain, they indulge in smiles and considerable criticism of one who arises in the camp, and speaks of a fire-encircled Summit, where blessed truths were engraven by God's finger on the tables of the heart. They overlook the spiritual meaning in the toilsome ascent of the mountain, the loneliness of the top, the waiting for days on God to reveal Himself. In a word, they neglect the conditions of obtaining Divine manifestations and blessings, and yet cry out against the statements of those who have fully obeyed these higher demands of the gospel.

If the Christian, descending to the camp from the fire-crowned mount, would only wear a veil, or if he would live his experience without any oral testimony, all would be well. It is the tongue that seems to hurt so in certain circles. Therefore, be it resolved, that, whosoever shall claim that he has received from Heaven anything different from, or superior to, the ecclesiastical circles of his village, town, or city,—behold! he shall be smitten at once upon the mouth. Be it, also, resolved that, whosoever shall strike this same offender with weapons of ridicule, misrepresentation, and oppression, he shall be counted to have done the Church a kindness, and rendered a service to God.

So the smiting goes on.

The sound of the blows are all over the land. The last few years reveal a vision of blood. Clenched hands are lifted, and fall with sickening thud upon mouths testifying to the truth; and the blood spurts.

What if this is a figure? Which is the more painful, a blow on the face, or private letters, published articles, and public deliverances where ridicule and unjust condemnation abound, and the thing struck at is not the face, but the man's reputation, influence, standing, work, and happiness. The bruised face will be well in a day or so; but what about the heart and life that have been struck? A cool linen bandage may heal the one; but who can undo the hurt of a written or printed lie? Can the writer himself do it? Who is willing to undertake such a journey and such a task, where the paper containing the misrepresentation or fabrication has a circulation of from ten thousand to five hundred thousand copies?

This slayer of his brother forgets that God asked Cain where his brother Abel was. This smiter of the Christian testifier forgets that God watches the fall of a sparrow, much more that of a falling hand, whose destination is a mouth that God made, and that is declaring what God, in His glorious power, has done and can do for the soul. He has also forgotten that God is a just God, and that this very fact of Divine justice and judgment will close the windows and doors of heaven upon him, and transform the sky into an impenetrable ceiling of brass. Prayer, like smoke, is driven back into the eyes of such a man, and communion with heaven without repentance becomes impossible.

In a word, this man, under a closed heaven, is now in fine condition to misunderstand, and even be wrathful with a child of God who speaks of open skies, descending doves, and flaming tongues of fire.

So it comes to pass that, look when and where we will, there is a vision of clenched hands, smitten mouths, and spurting blood. Blood is everywhere!

It is an age of blood-flowing, not simply in the military world, where swords and cannon are used, but in the after-history of investigation, where no position of responsibility and prominence will save a man from violent attacks. The vision of blood is in the political world, where one party spends most of its time in belaboring the other. It is in the commercial world, where, with every conceivable art, stratagem, and power, individuals as well as corporations are trying to undo and destroy some real or fancied opponent. It is in the literary world, where criticism is as keen as the blade of the guillotine, and as pitiless and unjust as the men who ran that instrument of death in the Reign of Terror.

When we come to the ecclesiastical world, the Church life, and, closer still, to the Christian life, we would expect and crave to see something different and better. But the vision of blood remains. Angry, clenched hands and crimsoned mouths abound. Religious denominations are still seen firing at each other, and chasing one another, as they do in war.

Two divisions of one great common creed are still debating about how to meet each other with amity and brotherly kindness in their work, and failing to do it. One of these bodies sends a delegate to the other to convey greetings. He does so, and sits down, when, in fifteen minutes, a leading man on the other side tomahawks and scalps him so quickly and cleverly in a platform reply, that the victim scarcely realizes that he has been slain. The great warrior sits down, with the scalp of the young chief at his belt, who, covered with blood, has hardly yet comprehended what has been done.

Look at the Church members striking at one another. Hear the stewards talking about one another. Listen to the preachers and evangelists judging, criticising, and condemning one another. See how the editors of Church papers are forever after one another. It is a vision of blood everywhere! It is a spectacle of cutting and slashing, stabbing and shooting, tomahawking and scalping, gouging and biting, wherever you turn. Doubled fists, smitten mouths streaming with blood, are on all sides. Heenan and Sayers, Sullivan and Kilrain, and Corbett and Fitzsimmons never gave harder and crueler blows in their line than I have seen and heard given in the name of Christ in this so-called Christian land.

We do not allude to warnings of and denunciations

against sin that must be delivered from the Church press and pulpit, but to personal attacks, the violent assailing of individuals who love God, and are keeping His commandments.

Listen to some of the words as they fall from the lips of the smiter as he strikes the mouth of one of God's Spirit-filled servants.

"He is not my style of preacher"—Smash!

"He does not cast out devils like I do. Hit him!"—Smash!

"He believes in the second coming of Christ, and is a visionary. Hit him, somebody—hit him, everybody"—Smash!

"He believes that Christ can heal the body"—Smash!

"He says, he has received the blessing of sanctification as a work clear and distinct from his regeneration. Let everybody strike him!"—Smash! smash! smash!

"He is a Church-splitter—a crank—a schismatic—an abuser of the Church and his brethren." Bang—thud—smash!

"Did you hear him?"

"No; but somebody else did."—Smash!

"Did you investigate the Church-splitting matter, and hear the other side of the case?"

"No; and I do n't want to."—Bang!

"Would you condemn a man unheard? Is that just, or right, or Christ-like?"

"I have n't time to talk with you. Hit him there, some one! Strike him again! Knock him down! That's it! Smash—smash! Now, drag him down the street like they did Stephen! Beat him as he goes! Roll him over and over! Thrust him outside the walls! Now finish him! Bang—thud—smash—smash—smash! Is he dead? Quite dead? All right! Now let us open Conference with the reading of the thirteenth chapter of First Corinthians, or begin divine service by singing the hymn:

> "Blest be the tie that binds
> Our hearts in Christian love;
> The fellowship of kindred minds
> Is like to that above."

XIX.

THE SILENCE OF CHRIST.

MANY, in studying the life of Christ, overlook the sterner side of His character. They make Him nothing but love; invest Him with a forbearance that has no end; and rob Him of justice, judgment, and that ineffable dignity and grandeur belonging to Him as King of kings and Lord of lords. They fail to see that He who wept over Jerusalem, drove out men and animals from the temple with uplifted scourge and burning, indignant words, "Ye have made my Father's house a den of thieves." That, while He said, "Come unto me, and I will give you rest," He also proclaimed, "Behold, your house is left unto you desolate." That He who took little children in His arms, said to the religious teachers of that day, "Ye generation of vipers, how can ye escape the damnation of hell?" That He who sat down, and opening His mouth, taught the multitudes unweariedly for hours, was silent in the presence of certain characters, and would make them no answer whatever.

There is no contradiction in this course of Christ, but perfect moral consistency. The explanation of the varying conduct is found in the characters of the individuals before Him. The Savior has evidently more than one side to His personality. There is a way of obtaining an audience, and enjoying delightful communion with Him; and there is a life we can live which will make the skies empty, lock the gates of heaven at our approach, and cause the Son of God to maintain toward us an unbroken silence.

The dreadful fact of Divine silence is the thought present to the reader; and this unspeakable calamity we bring on ourselves.

Christ was notably silent to certain men. The Bible says that, under the questions they put to Him, "He answered not a word."

Christ is silent to some people to-day. Some are honest enought to confess the great woe; in other cases many see it. Whether in Bible times or to-day, this Divine silence is not arbitrary, but is invariably the result of something the man has done, or, deeper still, what the man has become. Light is also thrown on the matter in one of Paul's inspired statements, "If we deny Him, He will also deny us." He is to us what we allow Him or make Him to be. Beyond all doubt, the fact of Christ ceasing to speak to a human soul can be explained.

Christ was silent to Herod.

The Scripture says Herod was glad to behold Him

of whom he had heard much, and now hoped to see Him perform some wonderful work. But no interrogation that this corrupt, unprincipled man could put to Jesus elicited the slightest reply or even a recognition of his presence. He said nothing, and did nothing so that Herod marveled.

Christ had previously said of Herod that he was a fox. He had a low, cunning nature. On top of this was a vulgar curiosity to see Jesus, and behold him work physical wonders that would make him stare. To such a character the Divine Being is invariably silent. There is nothing to be said to such a man except Judgment Day words, and that time has not yet arrived.

The writer has been struck with the fact that, after a remarkable outpouring of the Spirit on a meeting, there is an immediate rush of a certain element in the community to the next service, who are brimful of curiosity to see what is going on; and invariably we have observed on such nights a notable absence of the Holy Ghost. He would not work to gratify such a lust of the eye, or speak to men and women in such a mental and spiritual state.

Again, Christ was silent to Pilate.

The Roman governor put many questions to Jesus, and charged Him to answer, but the Evangels tell us,

"He answered him nothing." Two replies, evidently given for the benefit of the world, make all the more remarkable Christ's silence to the individual.

The study of the Roman governor shows him to have been timorous, cowardly, time-serving, and unjust. It is hard to conceive of a blacker character than that of the man who sat in judgment upon Jesus Christ. He knew Him to be innocent, said he found no fault in Him, and yet sentenced Him to the most horrible death known to men. Who wonders that, to the numerous questions he propounded, the Savior made him no reply?

Still again, Christ was silent to the chief priests and elders.

Matthew says, "When He was accused of the chief priests and elders, He answered nothing." And Mark states, "The chief priests accused Him of many things, but He answered nothing."

Every one who has beheld and felt the power of character; who has looked across the great gap and chasm that yawns between virtue and vice, truth and falsehood, righteousness and unrighteousness, can thoroughly comprehend and appreciate the silence of Christ to these men.

All of us have met persons, whom to talk with is simply to waste words, and lose time. They have put themselves where reason, truth, revelation, and warning are all alike lost upon them. To such people we finally become utterly voiceless.

In addition to this, we all know how the presence of unsympathetic, uncongenial natures will freeze the powers of speech, and drive us into profound silence. The explanation of being strangely shut up to individuals, or before assemblies, can often be found right here, while the exquisite suffering of being compelled for years or a lifetime to be in the presence of moral opposites can easily be imagined. Of course, this leads to silence, long spells of silence, and whether in business or family life, only that conversation is indulged in which is absolutely necessary, or that is felt to be one's duty.

We know of a married couple who lived over twenty years in the same house, and never exchanged a single word in that time. Neither one was religious, but one had moral character, and the other had none. One day there had been a revelation of a hideous, unprincipled heart, and straightway a silence of twenty years fell in between the two.

If we contemplate a single feature of Pilate's character, his injustice, we can easily see that that alone would be sufficient to account for Christ's voicelessness before him. All of us have doubtless been thrown with people at some time in our lives who seemed utterly incapable of rendering us justice. No statement or explanation we could make them in self-defense or extenuation, would make them change their opinions or remove their prejudice.

I once wrote a number of letters to a prominent man in order to disabuse his mind from the effect of false reports of my work. I was slow to awaken to the fact, but the awakening came at last, that he was set in his judgment and conclusions, and would not be persuaded, though one rose from the dead. From that moment a profound silence fell on me toward him, so far as self-defense is concerned. No matter what is written or told him, I never utter a word.

Many a daughter-in-law has found out that her mother-in-law will always side with her son. And many a son-in-law has ceased to expect justice from the mother of his wife. Such is the power of natural laws and affections that the woman is unable to discriminate and render true judgment. She is so biased by heart and family ties that the son-in-law ceases to expect justice, and falls into silence in the presence of this familiar manifestation of character.

All these things we mention that we might see why it is that, in spite of loud calling, testifying, praying, and preaching, some people obtain no answer from Christ. The state of the heart is such, the character is such, that it is impossible for the Savior to speak to them.

If a supposedly virtuous woman was seen chatting pleasantly on all kinds of topics with a man who was a notorious, impenitent libertine, observers who have any knowledge of character would immediately conclude that the woman was not herself pure. There could be pity and sorrow in a true woman's heart over such a character, and a gospel warning might be given, but there could be no friendly social conversation.

If I regard iniquity in my heart, says David, the Lord will not hear me. So, far from answering us, God will not even hear us. In other words, the kind of character or life or heart we bring to God settles the question whether we will hear from Him or not.

There are individuals to-day, and a number of them were once Christians, to whom the Lord speaks no more. It is plainly evident to the practiced spiritual eye. They are receiving no messages from Him. They are speaking to a silent Christ. As long ago prophesied, "They will call, and I will not answer."

Who has not beheld these persons, both in pulpit and pew? And who has not heard them testifying, praying, and preaching, and yet no answer from the Son of God?

Saul, the first king of Israel, got into this dreadful place, and his cry was, "God has departed from me, and answereth me no more." He, by disobedience, had brought himself where the Divine Being quit talking to him. Jerusalem is in that state to-day. Let the traveler go to what is called "The Wailing Place," and listen to the heartbroken cries, and then look up at the empty heavens above, where dwells the silent God. He came to them, and offered them eternal life. They refused to listen to Him. He foretold them what would at last come upon them as people, city, and nation, that they would one day call, and there would be no answer. It has all come to pass. The nation has been scattered, the city is trodden under foot, the temple is destroyed, and their God is silent above them. He answers no more, neither by dreams and prophets, nor by Urim and Thummim, nor by any other way; they, by their own conduct, have made for themselves a silent God, one who speaks to them no more.

May God, in His mercy, save the reader from this unspeakable woe and calamity,—a silent Christ, a Savior who has ceased to answer!

And yet there are men in the pulpit to-day who are living under this curse. And there are men upon ecclesiastical official boards, and women prominent in Church work, and people religiously busy in many ways, to whom Christ never speaks. And, sadder still, there are men and women dying now, while we write these words, to whom Christ is utterly silent, and the despair in their breasts at this hour springs from the fact that they made Him silent.

Again we repeat, May God save us from the immeasurable woe, both in life and death, of a silent Christ!

XX.

WAITING ON THE LORD.

THE Bible expression, "Waiting on the Lord," has several meanings according to the Scripture. One is that of service. So the Levites and priests were said to minister unto the Lord. Aaron, Eli, Samuel, Zechariah, and many others were found in the Tabernacle or Temple, actively engaged for God. It has a broader meaning to-day, and service to God can be offered not only in the church, but on street and highway, and wherever sickness, sorrow, pain, want, and sin can be found.

Another meaning is that of prayer. When men separate themselves from their pleasures and pursuits, and linger for hours and days in prayer for some special or general blessing, it is said to be a waiting on the Lord. So Moses on the Mount, Daniel by the river Hiddekel, Paul in the Temple, and the disciples in the Upper Room, waited on God. We do the same thing, whether at home or in the Church, when we plead for certain blessings and wait in supplication before the Throne.

A third meaning of the expression is a certain

tarrying on the Divine Providence. We wait to know the will of God in some steps of life, or to obtain explanation of an inscrutable divine dealing, or receive some peculiar deliverance, or enter upon the fulfillment of some divine promise.

This last waiting includes the other two. In order to tarry on God's time, the soul must abound in prayer, and be found in the divine service. To neglect either one would be to let go of the Savior, open the heart to doubt and worry, and end in the final forsaking of the post of duty where the Lord intended to have met and relieved us. Concerning this threefold waiting on the Lord, we have some blessed promises. Isaiah mentions four things as a certain result.

One is that we shall "renew our strength."

No argument is needed here to prove what has been felt a thousand times by the child of God. Something is found at the mercy-seat of prayer, and about the altars, and in the work of God, which is like new life to the soul. We come away from the closet of prayer and house of God with the feeling that we have been renewed or made over again.

Another promise is that we "shall mount up with wings as eagles."

The disciples took a great heavenward flight on the morning of Pentecost; but it was no accident. They had paid a great price for the privilege; they had waited ten days in the dust for the joy of putting the clouds under their feet.

Fletcher had upward soarings of religious experience, which many are fond of quoting, but not of imitating. Anyhow they will not pay the price he paid for his aerial ascents, which was four hours each day spent in prayer.

Some discuss with great gravity and scholarly acumen these wonderful uplifts in the kingdom of grace. They try to locate and then describe it in the realm of psychology, when the explanation is to be found in kneeology. A protracted waiting upon God will always be rewarded by the gift of a pair of wings. There is no shadow of a doubt upon the minds of observers when a Christian gets them. All can see he is mounting, and know he is far above the crowd that is standing by, gazing after him.

The experience of wings lifts the soul suddenly far above obstacles which just a moment before seemed insurmountable. The experience also gives a wonderful view of terrestrial things, God's works enlarging and man's works looking exceedingly small. Such caught-up people have also blessed things to tell us of Christ and His Kingdom. They seemed to have been near the Gates of Pearl. Let no man condemn them who never had a pair of wings given to his soul after days of importunity.

A third promise is, we "shall run, and not be weary." Have we not seen these people? They are always going for God, going swiftly, and that without seeming to be exhausted. They make no complaints, seem to have no dyspepsia or nervous prostration, and all they crave is the privilege of running for heaven. This man does not say so much about visions and views and great revelations; he is too busy running for God, delivering His messages, charging the enemy, executing flank attacks as well as front movements, picking up the wounded, distributing lint, making constant captures, and doing many other things too numerous to mention.

A fourth promise is, that we "shall walk, and not faint." It is placed almost last as the result of waiting on the Lord; but it is not less blessed than the other two, and may be even more important.

In these words a great multitude of the quiet, patient, faithful followers of Christ are presented. Men in the treadmill of every-day work, women in the toil and drudgery of home life. People so circumstanced that they can not run, but have to walk. So many hours for labor, so many mouths to fill, so many little garments to make, so many little ones to teach, so many small duties to perform.

When men with handspikes uplift a great log, they do not run, but walk, and with a slow, steady motion. There are some situations in the Christian life, and some duties where we can not run, but are compelled to go slowly. The load is heavy; it requires patience, deliberation, and steadiness, and will not allow swiftness. Thank God that heaven has a blessing for these quiet-lipped, grave-eyed, life-burdened followers of Jesus! We can walk through all, and not faint. It comes by waiting on the Lord.

An additional promise to the man who waits on the Lord is, that "he shall inherit the land." In another place David says, "He shall exalt thee to inherit the land." The figure is one of complete deliverance, perfect victory, and quiet establishment. Enemies are removed, ownership and mastership is given, and peace reigns supreme.

This last promise is made to the man who will wait on the Lord in the sense of tarrying for the Divine providence, or giving God His own time to do for us what we have asked and He has promised. It is a mark of great advancement in spiritual things when a man can do this. Many try it and break down; but some go to the end. Happy is such a man or woman of God. They shall be repaid and blessed beyond words to describe.

Some of us are marvelously inconsiderate here. We forget that when we ask God for certain things

He has to deal with others as well as ourselves, and always with free agents. He can not compel any one, but has to work with them in full recognition of their moral freedom.

The angel told Daniel, in explanation of a delayed message from heaven, that he had been withstood by a certain Prince, and hence prevented from coming.

It is a reasonable thing to wait on the Lord. It is what we want others to do for us. Sometimes we can not explain ourselves; sometimes our plans are working, but the consummation has not come. So we ask people to wait on us. If they love and trust us, they will. In like manner we pray God to bring certain things to pass. At once He starts the influences which are to prove successful; but it takes time. Many hearts and lives have to be touched and changed. Then God has plans of His own, which we do not see. He has to work them out, while at the same time He does not forget us, our past prayers, and present waiting before Him. Beyond all question He is doing His best for us. His answers and deliverances are on the way to us, struggling through human and Satanic opposition. Be patient a little while longer, ye heartsick children of God. It will yet come to pass, and you shall inherit the land.

The man of desperate acts takes things in his own

hand. The suicide took matters in his own hand. The people who flew to the wine-cup, the morphine-bottle, to the world, and into sin, would not wait on God.

The papers speak of a man who committed suicide on account of poverty. The next day a large remittance came by mail; but he was in his grave, and had placed himself there.

It pays to wait on God. Joseph looked at a closed prison-door for years. Doubtless his heart often sickened; but he waited on the Lord. One day the door opened, and Joseph not only walked out free, but was exalted to rule over the land.

John Wesley had a curse in his life. He neither committed murder nor suicide, as some men have done under similar circumstances. He waited on the Lord. The time came when the Lord completely delivered him.

One day in California, while sitting in a restaurant, I heard a man call for his dessert and a cup of coffee. The waiter tarried a little too long, he became impatient, jumped up, stamped out, and slammed the door. Just as the door closed behind him, and his feet were on the pavement, the waiter came in, bearing a delicious dessert and a fragrant, steaming cup of coffee. We have often since then thought of the simple scene. It was a parable in itself in spite of its simplicity.

The Lord keep us patient, faithful, steadfast. May we believe in, and rely on, and wait for Him! He has not forgotten us. Angels are on the way with nectar and ambrosia. Above all, God is coming with deliverance and blessing and honor and exaltation, and says meanwhile for our comfort that even now all things are working together for our good if we but love Him.

XXI.

THE CLEANSING BLOOD.

IN the Old Testament God took a world of pains to teach men that the cleansing of the soul could only be had through blood. This was the explanation of the red life-currents which streamed from bird, lamb, and bullock in the Jewish days. The meaning of the many sacrifices was, that without the shedding of blood there could be no remission of sins.

The next step was to show what or whose blood was meant. So, under the combined teaching of priest, prophet, and religious ceremony, the intelligent Israelite got to know that it was not possible for the blood of bulls and goats to purge the soul from the defilement of sin, that a nobler sacrifice was typified, and a more precious blood was yet to be poured out for the human race.

In due time the great antitype appeared, and died on Calvary. He suffered without the gate to sanctify the people. The Fountain was opened up in the House of David for sin and uncleanness. The means for perfect heart-cleansing, for snowy whiteness of soul, for complete purification from all sin, had come at last. Though one had lain among the pots, yet now should his wings be as burnished silver and his feathers like yellow gold. Not only should the soul be made white as snow, but whiter than the snow. The blood of Christ was to do it.

About this precious, blessed blood John has several things to say in his first epistle.

First, that it cleanses.

This is certainly an all-important statement, for many have been and still are looking in other directions for the longed-for purification. The eye has been fixed on Time, Old Age, Church Membership, Good Resolutions, Growth in Grace, and upon many other things to obtain that whiteness and cleanness which every soul must at times long for, and must also possess in order to see God.

But John says that it is the blood that cleanseth. This God-inspired announcement ought to save millions from countless and heartbreaking mistakes. There is absolutely nothing in any one of the things just mentioned to purify the heart. Whoever trusts to them is a fool, and doomed to bitter disappointment.

The Bible says, "The blood cleanseth." Myriads are shouting this in the sky, and multitudes are proclaiming it on earth.

There is no need to stop and explain to certain critical classes the difference between the procuring cause, the meritorious cause, the instrumental cause, and all the other niceties and hairsplitting definitions seen by scholarly minds in the plan and process of redemption. The great, blissful fact is, that the blood of Christ cleanses. This truth alone makes the sinking, despairing heart leap for joy, and turns the confused mind from its wanderings through a labyrinthian maze of theological, psychological, and diabolical error, and shows it, in a word, where and when and how spiritual cleanness can be found. But the apostle states another fact about the blood.

It cleanses from all sin.

This goes even beyond the first statement in its revelation of the depth and power of Christ's redemption. Many have brought part of their sins to God, but not all. Many believe that they have committed some things which can not be pardoned; that they have sinned away their day of grace; that their souls have been hurt irremediably by their own conduct; and that they are now doomed and certain to be damned.

All this gloomy talk is nothing but an emphatic denial of God's own Word, that the blood of Christ cleanses from all sin.

When God says a thing is so, what can man say after that? Is God a liar? Would He deceive a soul with false hopes? Do not all see that neither one is possible? Then if all sin can be cleansed by the blood, what need for any one to be in gloom or despair?

Let men say what they will, the Bible states that all sin is washed away. The guilty individual may cry out, "You have no idea what I have done." My reply is, "I do not care what you have done; the Scripture says that the blood cleanses from all sin." But the rejoinder is, "I have done thus, and so and so." All right, the blood cleanseth from all sin.

Once, while quite sick at home, a lady requested an interview. Her apology for insisting on seeing me when I was physically prostrate, was that she was in great spiritual darkness and agony of mind. I can never forget the anxious, distressed face of the visitor as she said:

"I am in darkness. For the love of God point me to a passage in the Bible that will save me from despair."

Sick as I was, I felt my face kindling with joy as I repeated, "The blood of Jesus Christ, His Son, cleanseth us from all sin."

"O," she replied, "that is so sweet!" And in a few moments went away with a bright countenance. But the adversary flung another cloud upon her the next day, blacker than the first. This time she went directly to the Bible, crying out, "Lord, let my eye fall on some word of thine which will bring me light, victory, and complete deliverance." Suddenly, as she read on, this verse fairly flashed itself before her eyes, "When I see the blood, I will pass over you." The result of a single reading was instantaneous and permanent relief.

A few months after this I was going from New York to Boston. The conductor came to me on the train, and, according to custom, wanted my fare. I handed him my ticket, which I had bought, and he gave me instead a small, red slip of cardboard, which I stuck in my hatband, and then placed the hat in an iron hatrack on the wall. At the next town quite a number of people got off, and another crowd came on. The conductor, not knowing me, approached where I was sitting and reading, and wanted my railroad fare. In reply I looked up and pointed to the red slip in my hat, whereupon he instantly passed by. This happened several times, until finally, begrudging even a few moments from the book in which I was immersed, the next time he came by and asked for my money, I never raised my eyes from the volume, but silently pointed with my finger to the little red card in my hat. The effect on him was always powerful. Invariably he passed me by without saying anything. In a word, when he saw the red, he passed over me. The little incident threw a gracious light on the Old Testament passage, and it became more precious and real than ever.

God, help us to believe. No matter what the mistake, mishap, error, or sin may be; may we have faith enough in the Bible and in the atonement to sprinkle the blood upon it. God's promise is, that when He sees the blood He will pass over.

A third statement of the apostle is equally remarkable and comforting. The blood cleanses from all sin while we are walking in the light.

This statement is more important than many dream, who hastily read the Scripture.

Numbers are contending to-day that regeneration is purity, that no sin is left in the converted heart. But this passage in John declares to the contrary. Mr. Wesley says it is one of the strongest verses in the Bible to teach the second work of grace.

If the reader will observe, John says that the man who obtains this peculiar heart-cleansing from all sin is in the light, is walking in it, and has fellowship with his Christian brethren. Here is a picture, not of a sinner, but of a child of God. He is in the light, is evidently growing in grace, is moving forward all the time, is in loving communion with other Christians, and right there the blood of Christ cleanses him from all sin. Moreover, the sacred writer says that it is "sin," not "sins," that he is cleansed from. The conclusion being unanswerable that a sin principle is left in the heart of the man who is walking in the light; in other words, that the Christian did not obtain purity in regeneration; but something is left which requires the blood of Christ to purge and deliver him from.

A fourth comforting teaching of the verse written by John is seen in the immediate appropriation of the blood by the regenerated or sanctified child of God, in case of neglect of duty or positive transgression. The word to believing souls at such a time is sweeter than the thrilling note of the silver bugle which announced the dawn or birth of the year of jubilee. "The blood of Jesus Christ, His Son, cleanseth us from all sin."

Deplorable as it is to fall into sin, yet God never intended that we should sink in paralyzing despair and perish, in case of the wrong thought, word, or deed. He would have His grieving child instantly confess all to Him, promise to be more faithful in the future, and believe that the blood of Christ cleanses him from this most humiliating of sins, a sin committed after the reception of grace and light, and Christ had become the Lord and Master of the heart and life. Thank God, the blood cleanses even then and there!

The fifth thought of comfort in the verse is that

the blood cleanses now. The verb is in the present tense. It does not say that the blood will cleanse; but that it does cleanse; it cleanses now.

Then if it cleanses now, why should one wait a week, day, hour, or a single minute for the soul's purification and restoration.

This one verse dashes to pieces the old Dark Age Theology, where Time, Bodily Humiliation, Peter's Pence, and Pilgrimages were invested with atoning, saving, and sanctifying power, and so Christ was robbed of His glory. To this day evangelical Christianity is burdened with these old, false Middle Age teachings.

There is nothing in bodily mortifications, and the flight of years to cleanse the soul. It is all right to groan and humble ourselves; but it is the Blood, after all, that can alone cleanse; and, thank God! it cleanses now! The instant that the soul really believes this, light, joy, and deliverance is sure to come. If the blessed fact is turned upon any sin in the life, or all sin, it is bound to go. If directed against the sin which remaineth in them who are truly regenerate, who are walking in the light, that also will as speedily and consciously depart; the Holy Ghost not only bearing witness to it, but the soul of the man himself all conscious of the departure. Here is where men are falling or rising to-day. Here is where they are floundering or flying. It is as they have read and received this marvelous Bible passage.

If our faith can not grasp the wonderful statement made in it, then, of course, we are shut out of its blessedness, for Christ can do no mighty work where there is unbelief. If we do not believe that the blood of Christ can destroy and take away inbred sin, He can not do it. But if we can and do believe that He can, and that He does, then, all glory and praise to God! the blood cleanses us now from all sin. He Himself has uttered the amazing words, "According to your faith, so shall it be unto you." Faith is not only the condition of salvation, but the measure of salvation. Again, Christ speaks, and says, "All things are possible to him that believeth."

Well might men say, after this utterance, "Lord, I believe!" Why should they with tears add, "Help thou mine unbelief." Faith honors God, faith pleases God, and faith in the power of the blood to cleanse now from any and all sin, will bring the blessing desired down upon the soul every time, and world without end.

XXII.

DWELLING AMONG LIONS.

SOME Scripture passages can only be unlocked by experience. We may think we understand; but it requires more than a knowledge of grammar, rhetoric, and the laws of exegesis to clear up the mystery.

When David said that his soul had dwelt among lions, a child's idea at once would be that he had been in the woods with wild beasts. This interpretation with the flight of time disappears, and something of the truth dawns upon the mind; but the wholeness of it remains for the deeply spiritual heart to comprehend.

It is not long in the Christian life before the child of God discovers the lions which David speaks of, and he will freely confess that for some reasons the animals of the forest would be pleasanter companions.

One of the dreadful facts about souls which depart from God into sin, is the steady and unmistakable drift into the habits, lives, and, finally, the appearance of animals. The devil, who is a fallen spirit, is called a serpent and dragon, and with profound reason for such nomenclature. The gravitation of ten thousand devils is seen first to be in the coarse, brutal animal nature of a demoniac, and then from him into a drove of hogs.

When human souls cut loose from God, the drift to the animal life is sure and evident. Music, literature, and other things may retard the progress somewhat to human eyes; but the awful undertow is there, and the man is being steadily carried out to the sea of fleshly grossness and carnality. The forces in the man's will and pursuits, and in the refinement of the social circle, are felt by and by not to be equal to the strange power which is dragging the spirit from likeness to God, and sinking it into the habits, ways, appetites, selfishness, and groveling existence of an animal.

Another curious thing is, that such men and women do not adopt one type, but fall, almost insensibly to themselves, into every variety of animal life known to man. So, in looking upon the multitudes of earth, we see not only lions, but wolves, foxes, hogs, goats, monkeys, snakes, and all the rest of the human menagerie. I hardly need ask the reader if he has seen men and women who have impressed him in appearance and ways with the animals just mentioned.

Neither jeans nor broadcloth can hide the hog at the table who evidently is not eating to live, but living to eat. A wolf looking at a lamb is a familiar spectacle in society. The human monkey who lives to be laughed at is in every neighborhood. And who has not seen the eyes of the fox fastened on you in office, parlor, or church; and felt the crawly approach of the snake, the touch of whose hand and soft, slippery style of speech created a sickening sensation similar to that when a serpent is discovered to be near.

These horrible likenesses instantly disappear under the regenerating and sanctifying power of God; and in this fact we obtain the second proof of what has been stated, that a spirit, human or angelic, which departs from God becomes animalized.

David's affliction was in being compelled to dwell awhile among men whom he could best describe as lions. He may have been thinking only of the ferocity of the beast; but it is doubtful. The full photograph reveals a catlike approach, treacherous waiting, the sudden spring, terrible roar, crushing blow, grinding teeth, tearing claws, and all the vast strength and cruel nature of the great brute of the forest.

With such men as Saul and Doeg to deal with, and such characters as Joab, Abishai, Ahithophel, and Shimei about him, the noble, magnanimous, spiritual David felt the repugnance and suffering analogous to one condemned to dwell with wild animals in the wilderness.

Christ knew what it was to be among lions when He looked into the pitiless faces of the high priest and elders, as He stood arrested and bound before them. He also saw as well as felt them in the dreadful treatment He received from the hands of a brutal soldiery, by whom He was tormented for hours through the night.

Paul was among lions when he stood before the Sanhedrim, or confronted the Jewish populace as, enraged over his religious experience, they cast dust in the air and howled for his death.

A Christian has lived a very obscure and solitary life who does not in time get to know the awful depths in the expression, "dwelling among lions." All of us have been among the lions. Some only for a little while; but others, through God's providence, have to abide with them a long time.

All will agree that for a child of God to be compelled to stay several hours in a room filled with drinking, gambling, cursing men, would be like being cast among lions. But the meaning goes deeper still. The verse has profounder and more painful applications.

It is to live year after year in a godless community, where Christ is forgotten, the Sabbath desecrated, the Bible and religion laughed at, while the devil is the unquestioned monarch and ruler of the place. The actual sight of lions rolling over each other, now gamboling and playing, and now fighting each other with fearful roars and gaping wounds, would not be a more dreadful spectacle to behold than what many of God's children are compelled to witness from day to day and year to year, in towns and cities that seem utterly given up to every kind of folly and sin.

Dwelling among lions is to be a member of a cold, dead, formal, worldly congregation, where a conversion never takes place, where genuine revivals are laughed at and denounced, where the class-meeting is abandoned, and the church given over to lectures, Chautauquan circles, church suppers, ice-cream festivals, grab-bag performances, and every conceivable kind of amusement.

Dwelling among lions is to be a member of a Conference Synod, Presbytery, or Council, where no one believes that God can and does sanctify the soul instantly in answer to consecration, prayer, and faith. The roar and rending that takes place over such a testimony and Church report will show that all the lions are not dead yet.

It is to stand up in some Preachers' Meeting and claim the experience of entire sanctification, and gently urge the blessing upon others. The sight of a half-dozen persons springing, so to speak, at the testifier's throat in loud and angry denial, will throw considerable light on David's words, "My soul hath dwelt among lions."

It is to sit in a car, stage-coach, or at a hotel

table where escape is impossible, and be compelled to listen for minutes or hours to the profanity or obscenity of young traveling agents.

It is to be a member of an irreligious household, and feel as lonely and even lonelier than Robinson Crusoe on his island, or a hermit in the desert.

It is to be united for life to a man or woman whose unspiritual, carnal, or worldly life makes a gap and chasm between the husband and wife, like that between a man and an animal. There are mutual, instinctive shrinkings from each other, as a man would draw back from an animal, or an animal would depart from a man. But the laws of God and the State are such that the ghastly companionship can not be broken.

Again, the experience is seen in being thrown with very disagreeable religious people. They claim the nature of the sheep; but keep up the old-time roar, the slash of the claw, the bite of the tooth, and the heavy blow of the paw. It seems impossible for them to let a person come into or leave their presence without inflicting a gaping wound. "The sermon was wrong," "the exegesis was faulty," "the manner was not pleasing," "the voice was too loud," "the dress was objectionable," and so on, endlessly. They are self-commissioned to set everybody right but themselves. They have slaps, scratches, bites for all their brethren and sisters, which they call heavenly rebukes and revelations. They are Divinely appointed to go around and tell everybody how to dress and who to marry, and how to do generally. They have received a revelation from God that it is wrong for a man to wear a mustache, while women must wear Mother Hubbard-looking dresses, and let their hair hang down their backs like the mane of a Shetland pony. They have, moreover, just received some new light, with some new notions, and everybody must come right over into their way of thinking, or take the consequences of going at once into backsliding, and finally into hell.

Again, the lions are seen in the shape of argumentative and disputatious, religious people. They look in the midst of their pulpit, platform, and pen deliverances, not to say attacks, as if they were after mashing and killing a man, instead of saving him. Everybody is wrong, and they are right. They have just received the last edition of the Bible from heaven. The world is getting worse all the time; Saturday is the true Sunday; Turkey and the whole Mohammedan Empire was to go down in 1898; and whosoever will not believe and receive these things ought to be kicked out of the community and sent to hell in a body. This is just the way it looks and sounds.

Still again, the lions are beheld in the form of

untidy religious people. The apology made for them is that they are eccentric. The plain truth in English is, that in body and apparel they are unclean. We expect nothing better of lions, for they have neither soap nor towels, and have to wear one suit for a lifetime. But there is no excuse for human beings, with springs and rivers flowing around them in great numbers and overflowing abundance, while soap can be had for a cent a bar.

It is a great mistake to quote the wild life and rough manners of John the Baptist, and the unkempt condition of Elijah as God's idea of a man's life and appearance. These two men were great, not because of these things, but in spite of them. The Baptist is not heaven's conception of the perfect man, with his shaggy mantle, food of locusts, almost clotheless body, and generally ascetic life.

Jesus Christ is the ideal man! With his tunic, sandals, and the garment woven without a seam, He was well clothed. And He came eating and drinking. He was the sound, wholesome, morally symmetrical man, who is worshipped around the world to-day, and is drawing all men unto Himself. The children were not afraid of Him, but nestled in His arms; the women sat at his feet; the sick and troubled flocked to Him, and as the Pharisees themselves said, "Behold the whole world is gone after Him."

XXIII.

THE BLESSINGS OF TIME.

TIME is a segment cut out of the rim or circle of Eternity. It is a kind of projection or loop from an endless line. It comes out of the eternal as an infinitesimal part of it, and is to be swallowed up by it as a raindrop falls back into the ocean, from which it was originally lifted. The angel with uplifted hand foretells its approaching funeral, and declares in trumpet tones, "That there should be time no longer."

But with all its comparative littleness as to duration, what tremendous events have transpired and will yet occur between its two gates—the Beginning and the End. The creation of a race is seen, its thrilling history of sin, sorrow, defeats, redemption, struggles, victories, death, resurrection, and the final judgment and everlasting division into the Lost and Saved. Then comes the closing scene of the heavens rolling up, the earth on fire, Satan cast into hell, and Christ victorious over all for evermore.

To the individual life and history, time is scarcely less momentous, for it brings to each soul the very things that have come in a colossal scale to the world. Between the cradle and the grave each man and woman is made to realize the fact of two other worlds besides this, that are contending for the soul; the one to pull down and destroy, and the other to uplift and save. Sin, sorrow, sickness, failure, suffering in many forms, come to all. So, also, does salvation appear, with pardon, peace, purity, usefulness, happiness, and blessedness in its hands, as gifts to the believing, obedient soul.

To some, time is only a curse and a burden through lives of evil. They are glad to get rid of it. There are others who not the less feel the sorrowful load which the years bring to the mind, heart, and body, but through Christ have learned to endure all patiently, in hope of an immortal crown and joys that never die beyond the grave.

There is still a third class who, not the less sensitive to the ills, pains, hardships, disappointments, mortifications, crosses, and troubles which are necessarily connected with an earthly existence, yet have made such discoveries through the teaching of the Spirit, that they plainly see how time, under God's blessing, is a friend to grace, and does through Divine power what nothing else could possibly do.

One thing it brings to the true child of God is the spirit of moderation.

The force of a devoted Christian life, for all its desirableness, is not without peril. A stationary engine, as it lies sidetracked without coal, water, or fire, is helpless and useless. We have plenty of such in the Church to-day. But an engine trembling with a mighty head of steam needs a steady hand and level head at the throttle; for some have gone too fast, some run beyond the depot, some pitch down a bank, and others are blown up.

There is a danger of an intolerant, arbitrary, and even fierce spirit creeping into the hearts of the newly converted and sanctified, under the mighty inflow of Divine glory and power. The conservation and proper direction and use of this great spiritual force is not at once learned by them. The boiler is injured at times by heatings not commanded of God, the bell and whistle terrifies and paralyzes rather than warns, and sometimes people are run over who might have been saved. The cowcatcher is put at an angle, not so much to lift up as to grind and crush. People are grieved whom God has not grieved.

Other Christians have as much steam as the fiery, new engine on the road; but have distributed it evenly on the gospel train, so that not only is a proper speed kept up, but the passengers are made comfortable as well; while the new locomotive is mindful mainly of its whistle and high rate of running, and its passengers, missing certain genial, heavenly, Christ-like influences that should stream backward in proper channels, slowly freeze.

The new engine is apt to indulge in caustic remarks at the expense of the older locomotives, albeit some of them for many years have maintained the unbroken record, "On Time."

The only hope for the case just mentioned is to be found in what Christ will be able to do through time. Nothing else can do it—light, argument, exhortation, warning, example, and even the Divine patience and pity, will not effect the change from intolerance and arbitrariness to a spirit of gentleness and moderation. But time, through grace, will do it. The man will little by little see his honest, intellectual mistakes, his misjudgments of men, and his erroneous conceptions of truth and duty. What a relief all around!

Great spiritual light poured into the mind does not always mean that the head is wise and the judgment will be infallible. Then, again, we can not read the hearts of men. Some people do not parade all they are doing for God and man. In every Church I have served as pastor, there were individuals who would never give publicly, nor even sign a card; but nevertheless they contributed a great deal more than some who cried out in tones that could be heard all over the Church, "Put me down twenty-five dollars!"

I once thought a man was niggardly; but found afterwards he was supporting two preachers in a foreign land, and saying nothing about the matter.

Little by little with time the eyes get open. Our lips are not as ready with criticism and judgment as of yore. With no less zeal for God and His cause, yet it is now a zeal according to knowledge. The moderation is not a cooling off of religious experience, nor a curtailing of work, nor a withholding of testimony. It is, instead, a deliverance from hastiness of judgment, jumping to conclusions, and quickness to suspect and speak hardly and severely of others. It is the departure of a domineering, autocratic spirit and manner. It is the correcting of pure love, the mellowing of the Christian into a calm-eyed, level-headed, sweet-hearted, kindly-tongued man. He is as true to God and the gospel as ever; but all the more true in that he has learned to be undeviatingly kind to men whom God made and Christ died for. He has the spirit of moderation.

A deeper apprehension of what we mean is to be had by contrasting the counsel and speeches of young men on the floor of Convention and Conference, with the utterances of the older men. A second illustration is beheld in the loquacity and bearing of a young graduate from a theological college when placed in charge of his first work, or in the company of men that he thinks have not had the advantages he has enjoyed.

An eminent man once said that, "Early in life as

a student I thought I knew everything; later, nothing; still later, something." Here was moderation.

Another man said in the beginning of his Christian life he thought everybody was white. Then, with certain revelations and experiences, he concluded all were black. Now he says all look gray. We judge that he meant he had found good traits in bad people, and objectionable things in good people, and so mixing his colors he got a neutral tint on his glasses with which he viewed the world. While not accepting all of his theology, yet it would be well to quickly recognize the good in all, and at the same time see if our own willfulness, headiness, quickness to judge and condemn, may not be the means of turning still other people into critics and judges of ourselves, and so cause them to think as they observe these dark lines against our white professions, that, after all, there is no pure white in the Christian life; that gray is all that we can hope for possibly.

Another blessing that comes with the flight of time is what I would call the outgrowing of certain things. Some of us remember when aprons and knee-pants were discarded; also when marbles and tops failed to interest us. As children we had hung breathless over the stories of "Robin Hood," "Robinson Crusoe," and the "Swiss Family Robinson." One day, when nearing the twenties, we took up the books and tried to read them, wondering where the charm was which once we felt in their pages. They now wearied us. There was still fascination in the books for a younger generation; but not for us, for we had outgrown them in mind, as our body had outgrown the little shirt-waists we once wore on the days we could walk under our father's dining-table without touching it with the top of our head.

The soul is constantly advancing and developing, and grows faster when properly treated. It is a pitiful thing to see it kept down to playthings and picture-books in the intellectual and spiritual life, when it ought to be grappling with the greatest truths and solving the deepest problems.

We have all noticed how people tire of various things after a few repetitions. They weary of certain amusements and accomplishments, become bored with visiting and visitors, and fagged to death with travel. Yet there was a time when these things were like Paradises to them. They still charm other novices for a while; but the older and wiser ones turn in other and new directions for contentment and satisfaction. The explanation is that the soul is still growing. Made for the illimitable and the eternal, how can this planet, with all that it contains, satisfy permanently a spirit that Christ says is greater than the world, and is always reaching out for something higher, mightier, and better than it has? So, by and by the world itself, with all its pleasures and pursuits, becomes an outgrown thing.

The idea of an individual going back on earthly routes for the satisfaction and filling of mind and heart, is as absurd as a man trying to wear the garments and read the books of boyhood days. He looks on the same scenes that once made his heart leap; but the heart never bounds again as it did at the first sight. He has outgrown and passed beyond them.

In the religious life we are told to leave the first principles, and to go on to perfection. This does not mean that we give them up in the sense of renunciation of their benefits and denial of their truth, any more than a man gives up the alphabet when he gets to reading, and takes up the study of history, art, and science.

We have been made to marvel at preachers spending years in the discussion of water baptism, laying on of hands, grades in the ministry, etc. Time was we tarried there; but we saw something better on ahead, and went on.

Some ministers are wedded to the ecclesiastical regalia of beaver hat and clerical coat. Others prefer to lay them aside, and do so without any condemnation of heart or lips of those who prefer the ministerial uniform. But in their hearts they feel they have in a sense outgrown the garb, and prefer to be recognized as Christ's servants in other ways.

Some delight in titles, and, as Christ says, love to be called Rabbi, Rabbi, in the market-places. The day comes when all these things, together with the semicircular row of chairs on the conspicuous platform, get to be exceedingly small, and become perfectly sickening to the soul.

Some rejoice in the red tape and machinery of the Church and Conference. Some delight in the office of Conference secretary, chairman of committees, and places on Boards of all kinds. Others have seen the Spirit in the wheels, have beheld a man's hand in the midst of the complex machinery which Ezekiel describes, and have had such a vision of a marred countenance with a crown of thorns on a blood-besprinkled brow, that they can not with any heart or willingness go back to anything that is less spiritual and divine. They have outgrown the old life, have cracked the shell and got the kernel, have stripped away the envelope, and stand thrilled with the sweet, heavenly handwriting they have found there.

Let those who love platforms, big occasions, public orations, chaplaincies, fraternities and lodges, fêtes and orations, Church lobbying and wire-pulling, secret meetings and councils, dignities and honors—let them go after them. We would not condemn them.

We only say that the soul, all-panting for Christ and Christ alone, has seen Him, and is in full pursuit, refusing to be diverted or turned aside by any object, and determined to settle on nothing less or lower than Jesus, the Son of God. The dead can bury the dead; he proposes to preach the gospel with the Holy Ghost sent down from heaven. Men may worship the Temple; but he is after the Lord of the Temple. Men may dispute and wrangle about the chief seats in the synagogue; they can have them all; he does not desire a single one; he is perfectly satisfied in sitting at the feet of the Savior. He craves no newspaper puffs and notices; wants no college complimentary degrees; fishes for no praise or flattery, and is not one particle hurt in being overlooked and set aside. The figure of the suffering, dying Christ on the cross has been burned into his soul by the baptism of fire, and weaned him forever from the littleness, hollowness, fussiness, swagger, and strut of life. For the first time he knows what Paul meant when he said, "Let no man trouble me; for I bear in my body the marks of the Lord Jesus;" and for the first time he goes to the very bottom of the hymn:

> "When I survey the wondrous cross
> On which the Prince of Glory died,
> My richest gain I count but loss,
> And pour contempt on all my pride."

XXIV.

THE FALL OF BALAAM.

THE word fall suggests the thought of height or position from which to be cast down. A man flat on the ground has nothing in a physical sense to fall from or fall to. The Bible says that Judas "fell," which quiet statement is sufficient to shut the mouths of those who say he never possessed redeeming grace. If answer is made that it is said he fell from the "apostleship," our reply is that the idea of Christ inducting an unconverted man into the ministry is simply unthinkable. Judas fell from the apostleship, which position means more than an office, and stands for spiritual light, life, and grace as well.

And so Balaam fell.

This means that he had something to fall from. That he was a good man to begin with, no thoughtful reader of the Bible or student of the human heart can deny.

In the first place he was a prophet. Not self-instituted; but God called and used. The fact of this ecclesiastical position shows that he was all right at first. He who said, "If the blind lead the blind, they both will fall into the ditch," will hardly be guilty of the inconsistency of placing an unconverted man over the unsaved. The preacher or prophet of God's choosing and ordination is bound to be a good man. He may fall away in after years; but when the call and installment take place, he is all right.

Two indications of Balaam's piety might be overlooked by the hasty reader. One appears in the statement that when the servants of Balak came with the request that he would come and curse a certain people that were covering the land, Balaam's prompt reply was that he would have to ask God. This unquestionably shows a close walk with the Lord. Let the Christian reader ask himself if the first impulse with him, and immediate practice, is to bring to God for guidance and approval everything that comes up in life in the way of duties, and especially matters of personal advantage.

We read that Balaam obtained an early reply from God telling him not to go with the men. This immediate answer from heaven is another striking proof of the man's acceptance and spiritual standing. Some who read these lines will recall how many hours have been spent by them on their knees awaiting light and a response from God in regard to certain steps of life. But there is a life where the soul gets constant and instant direction. Balaam in this first view of him seems to have been at that point, or, rather, on that high moral ground.

Up to this moment the man seems blameless, but after this we get an unmistakable glimpse of inbred sin and the peculiar direction it took in his case. Next day, we read, the servants of Balak returned with still greater urgings that he would come, and with assurance of reward. Right here is seen the inner trouble, "the ground of the heart" of the prophet, in his own words, that he would go in and see if the Lord would allow him to depart this time. Here at once flashes into view the "proneness to wander," the "bent to backsliding," which the Bible recognizes in God's people, and which the Lord wants to burn out with the baptism of the Holy Ghost and fire.

It should have been sufficient for Balaam that God had answered in the negative on the day before. God does not change, and if it was wrong for the prophet to go yesterday, it was wrong for him to go to-day. But the inclination toward a forbidden thing was already in him, and growing as well. Already his eyes were fastened on the "wages of unrighteousness," which, according to the apostle, wrought his ruin.

Some have wondered that the Lord permitted him finally to go. But he was no more allowed to do as he did than any Christian is sanctioned in wrongdoing. Man is a free moral agent, and can not be forcibly and physically restrained. When Christians go into sin, they realize that they have an indwelling power to do so, in spite of light, grace, warnings, rebukes, and protests from man and God. In this power Balaam went. The Bible says God went out to "withstand" him. He could not, consistently with the principles of His kingdom and the moral constitution of the man, bind him with ropes, imprison and in other ways keep him from departing, but He could "withstand him;" i. e., throw difficulties, obstacles, and warnings in his way.

And so an angel met him down the road with a flaming sword, and waved him back.

The "perverse" man, as the Bible calls him, went on. There are many like him to-day, the similarity being not only in wrongdoing, but in being divinely met down the road with warnings and swords of flame. When Christians receive strange and unexpected rebukes from human lips, and, at times, in letters, it is time to inquire in the life, and see if all is well.

Of course, a child of God may expect wrathful utterances from the world, and sharp lectures and faultfindings from religious oddities, croaks, and cranks. But if the remonstrance and warning come from really good people, the angel side of the world, there is cause for alarm. In the ghastly moral falls that now and then take place among Christians, the facts, if known, would be that they received solemn appeals and warnings from people of God, months and years before the life and character crash came.

It is curious to note that, in addition to the opposition of the angel, God added pain of a physical character to Balaam. The ass on which he rode became affrighted at the supernatural spectacle, ran into the wall, and ground the foot of the prophet against the stones. Balaam became infuriated, and smote the dumb beast, who actually saw more than the prophet did.

The physical pain always comes with the warnings of God. To stray out of the order of God's will and providence is to be continually getting hurt. Things go wrong. Accidents, as we call them, happen; all kinds of painful, unexplainable things take place.

In the case of a layman who began to depart from God, after a devout life, there occurred, one after another, such physical mishaps and narrow escapes of life that he became deeply alarmed, and flew back to duty and God.

Not all do this, but become filled with a blind rage against the very things and beings God sends to block their way to ruin, and go to striking right and left, and with a growing fury as the years go by, In a word, they begin to ripen for destruction.

Not only poor dumb animals feel the cruelty of

these maddened, backslidden lives, but innocent members of the family. Everybody seems to them to be blocking up their way, hindering them in their pleasures, pursuits, rights, and privileges; so down comes the cudgel of word, look, act, and life itself, on bleeding, faithful hearts. Is it not strange that all can see that God is dealing with them but themselves? Inferior minds and natures recognize the spotted record and doomed life, while he, the wrong and wandering one, frets over hindrances that have been sent of God, and pushes on to ruin.

Farther down the highway Balaam encountered the angel again.

The reader will notice the expression, "farther down," which we use. The second battle did not take place on the same ground of the first. God fell back as His perverse servant pressed on, and met him at a remote spot.

The idea is, that while the Lord keeps up the contest with the disobedient Christian for a while, yet the struggle is never on the same moral place or plane. As the soul pushes past God, who is making effort to stop and save it, that soul is compelled to become harder and worse for such a course. So the next warning and withstanding takes place, in a true sense, farther down the road. And the third battle is still farther down than the second, the man persisting in evil, God continuing to fall back and withstand him again, until the time is reached when the Lord steps aside, and allows the infatuated and determined man to go on to his destruction.

The disobedient Christian can tell that he is farther down the road, and in the last conflicts with Heaven, by the lessening power of conscience, and the rarer, fainter utterance of the voice of the Spirit. The man, however, becomes accustomed to providential hinderings, and looks upon them daily with less concern, and finally with no trouble at all.

There were three more Divine withstandings of the prophet on the top of the mountain, and each one occurred in a different place. God did His best to save Balaam, and put a blessing instead of a curse for His people into his unwilling lips.

The man said some fine things on the mountain standing by God's altar. It was the spiritual flaring up of the human candle before going down and out in the socket. He was ostensibly in the service of God; but the drift of his soul toward the forbidden evil had become now like the rush of Niagara just above the falls.

Samson and David went down under the power of women; Judas and Balaam fell through love of money. The former class of transgressors doubtless wonder how the latter class could so care for bits of shining metal. In like manner we doubt not that the metallites, or second class, marvel at the weakness of the first class, as they succumb to female arts and blandishments.

Nevertheless, both classes fell, and a fall is a fall, whether it be over a Bathsheba or a bag of money. Men are going to hell from both causes. Samson, David, Balaam, and Judas, all went down with a crash into sin. Where can be the comfort to any one in a moral fall in recalling that he did not go down like his neighbor, or with the sin of his neighbor? If a half-dozen men have fallen into a deep well, it matters not a particle whether they tripped over a rock or slipped on a piece of spongy soil; whether one was looking at a star, or another chasing a firefly; the grievous fact is that all are in the well. Think of a spirit of pride and boasting springing up in such a miry place as to the manner in which each one got there! The whole dispute would be absurd and profitless. So, when a man has fallen into moral ruin, what need to boast that he did not go down like his neighbor, or with the sin of his neighbor? He sinned, that is enough; and he is down, and that is more than enough.

Of the four individuals mentioned above, but one seems to have been rescued, and that one was David. The Scripture is unmistakable about the ruin of Judas and Balaam. They were wrecked on the money question.

There is a rapids in Niagara, not only below the falls, but one above. So is it in life. Just before a man takes the final leap into sin there is a marvelously accelerated movement in his life toward moral ruin that is plainly observable to many, and that corresponds to the Upper Rapids.

When Balaam left the mountain in the last work he did for God, he was in the Rapids. God evidently met him no more, but stood aside and let the man leap to his destruction. And he leaped, or was carried over the Falls, just as the reader prefers to regard the matter. The fallen prophet, fully determined to obtain the pay and honors of King Balak, does one of the most diabolical things on record in the Bible. Knowing, as he did, that the awful judgment of God would come upon the children of Israel if they carnally intermingled with the nations by the way, Balaam in some manner, according to the Bible, brought about the transgression between the men of Israel and the women of Moab. In this way the curse which he was not permitted to pronounce from the mountaintop was brought on the Israelites by their own act.

The man was now out of the Rapids and in the Falls! In a few days he had entered the Rapids below the Falls. He had, in a word, yielded to a rushing temptation, shot an awful downward plunge into the vortex of sin, and soon came to the place and hour when physical destruction was added to moral ruin, as the Lower Rapids in Niagara pound to pieces everything that is borne to it from the Falls.

The Bible tells us that a great battle took place as the result of what had gone before, in which conflict many were slain, and among the killed was Balaam, the unfaithful prophet of God.

May God have mercy on any one of His servants who has become careless in life, and commenced opening his heart to questionable thoughts, desires, and ambitions! As yet he is only floating on the stream, and almost imperceptibly; but he has left the place of safety, and from where we stand we can see the arrowy rush of the Upper Rapids of an increasing evil influence, hear the dull roar of the Falls of the sin itself, and see in the still remoter distance the gray, jagged rocks, and wild, leaping waves of the Lower Rapids, where disaster and physical death are certain to come. The heart involuntarily cries out for mercy in behalf of the drifting soul and doomed body of such a man. And yet what escape and deliverance can be expected for one who in steadfast perversity has fought his way through every warning and withstanding that a patient, loving God could devise and execute. Still we cry out, God have mercy!

XXV.

THE MAN NEAREST TO GOD.

IN Second Chronicles we read that a great multitude of the Ammonites and Moabites had gathered against Israel. The situation was so dark and hopeless from human view, that the people with their little ones were in humble supplication before the Lord. The king himself was no exception. All hearts were anxious, troubled, and looking to God.

In the midst of this protracted waiting, suddenly the Spirit of God fell upon a man in the congregation, whose name was Jehaziel. At once he opened his lips and uttered the most comforting and strengthening words to the Jews. He told them that God would deliver them, and that in a most remarkable way. He bade them be of good cheer, that they only needed to stand still, and they would see the salvation of heaven.

The fulfillment of the man's words will be remembered by the reader. So great was the victory which God wrought for His people, that they were three days gathering up the spoil.

From the circumstance of the Spirit of God falling upon Jehaziel we obtain the startling and thrilling truth that God in His work uses the man nearest to Him. This is not simply a gracious fact, but a most solemn one, and one calculated to stir the Christian heart to its profoundest depths. As a truth, it is not only taught in the Bible, but as constantly proved in life.

We have noticed merchants on busy days in their stores; observed managers and directors of work in a time of rush; and seen old-time masters with their slaves on sudden calls for immediate action; and invariably we have marked that the individual nearest to the merchant, overseer, or master was the one employed to do a work or commissioned to bear a message. We frequently saw this, but failed to be impressed with its deep significance when applied to spiritual things, until we brooded over the case of Jehaziel.

What we see men doing, the Lord does. He uses the human instrument that is nearest to hand. It is a principle of conduct which applies in both the business and moral world. No one who gives a thought to the matter but can and must approve. God uses the man closest to Him. This is the great truth of the passage! From it we draw several reflections.

First, the mystery is explained of the Divine favor and use of certain men in the Church and world.

People who have wondered why God blesses some

persons so abundantly, and why He employs them so constantly, need marvel no longer with such Scripture before them. The Divine Hand is laid on the nearest head. The Lord speaks to the man closest to Him.

Of course, there were good people in the congregation of Israel that day, as there are in religious gatherings to-day. But some were nearer to God than others. The good King Jehoshaphat was closer than the people; but Jehaziel was nearer still than the king. He was the nearest, and so on him the Spirit of God fell.

We have often beheld similar scenes in Sabbath audiences and revival-meetings. There are good people in the congregation, and some are better, and there is the man or woman who is best or nearest to God. On that soul the Holy Ghost is certain to descend. It is as fixed, unchangeable, and faithful a Divine procedure as God working in His great natural laws. Indeed, it is a law. Whoever stands nearest to God will be most blessed and honored of God. Nothing else can happen to one in such a moral position. Wonderful place of grace and glory! Who would not occupy it?

For sidelights to this blessed truth, let the reader turn to the description of the Last Supper, and observe that John heard the Savior say things which escaped Peter and the other disciples. The explanation was that he was nearest to Christ.

Let him look again on the banks of the river Jordan, and see the Dove alighting upon Him who spent whole nights in prayer, and who said, "My meat is to do the will of Him who sent me." To this day the Dove comes to the Lamb, to the soul most like Christ.

Another reflection drawn from the occurrence which befell Jehaziel, is that here is a Divine testimony to human faithfulness. The Spirit of God only falls upon prepared hearts.

This fact utterly demolishes the hope of spiritually lazy people, who expect to be blessed, and yet fail to put themselves in the heart, mind, and life position to be thus honored of God. They wonder why the glow they see in other faces is not in their own, and why the spirit buoyancy, inward exultation, liberated tongue, and unmistakable unction of life is not theirs. The explanation is that the condition of praying, life emptying, believing, and waiting has not been met by them. They have been spiritually indolent, have failed to plow, harrow, plant, and cultivate, and yet are looking for a waving harvest and full granaries.

Nothing is said in the passage about any special devotion of time and energy to God by Jehaziel; but the Bible has so clearly taught this to be the indispensable condition of spiritual manifestation and revelation, that to state God's Spirit fell upon the man is tantamount to saying that he had been waiting upon, and living close to God.

The flames of fire, shining countenances, and wondrous, rapturous utterances of Pentecost, were preceded by ten days of patient supplication to God in the Upper Room. The visions of Daniel came; but not without weeks of fasting and prayer upon his part on the banks of the river Hiddekel.

Some affect to be surprised and even hurt at the sudden outbursts of joy, and the Divine use of certain persons in religious services. Why not themselves? is the fretful query often asked inwardly, when not uttered to others. The answer has already been given, and is also embraced in the Bible statement—the man who prayeth secretly shall be rewarded openly. The private devotion is the explanation of public heavenly honor. The closet of prayer is the place where the crown and robe are obtained which make a man appear as a spiritual king when standing before the Church and world.

A young preacher rebuked a large company of gamblers on a steamboat with such holy power that it not only awed the men, but led the rebuker to a great national honor. The secret of his ascendency was that he had spent a couple of days in his stateroom in tears and prayer over the matter. Any one could have had a kind of brute courage sufficient to have condemned the transgressors, and still have accomplished nothing. This kind of reproof is cheap, and obtained at little cost; but few are willing to pay the price of two days' humiliation and prayer to secure the heavenly backing and the Divine favor and power this man possessed.

A prominent minister of the gospel ridiculed the doctrine of a second work of grace in a large concourse of people. There were many good persons present who disapproved his utterances, but could not or did not speak in reply. The Spirit fell that morning upon a young preacher to answer the denier of sanctification by faith in the blood of Christ. For thirty minutes by the clock this suddenly appointed defender of a great Bible truth fairly flamed and glowed in his presentation of the doctrine and proclamation of the experience, while love to man and gratitude to God was heard in every utterance, and tears of joy welled into his eyes and fell fast upon his cheeks. To many the thought doubtless came, that this man was a chosen instrument to protect the ark, and so settled back in the old condition of spiritual laziness. The real explanation was that the young preacher had spent several days in special waiting upon God. He, in other words, happened that morning to be nearest the Lord, and so the Divine Hand was laid upon him, with the command, "Speak for Me."

Nothing in nature occurs in a haphazard way. Law regulates everything. A Divine Hand guides and controls according to perfect wisdom, truth, and faithfulness. In like manner in the kingdom of grace there is nothing like moral accidents. The same God presides in both realms. Law is in both worlds.

We talk about the lightning striking at random. It is not so: the electric fluid falls on the object nearest to it, and most favorable for its reception. So does the heavenly lightning. The Spirit comes upon people who are prepared for Him.

A brief final reflection we draw is, that none of us can afford to miss standing in the place nearest to God. We can without much hurt be cast out of social circles, synagogues, and places of earthly honor; we can be displaced from favored positions near the rich and great; but we can not, without irreparable injury to ourselves both now and forever, live at a distance from God. We must for our present and future highest good stand close to the Heavenly King, where His hand can touch us, and His voice reach us at any and at all times.

It is this spot where is ever to be found the flaming speech, transfigured countenance, unctuous life, and beautiful influence, more powerful at times than words and deeds themselves.

Here John lived, and talked about opening heavens, and said, "Hear what the Spirit saith to the Churches." Here Paul abided, and spoke about not knowing whether he was in the body or out of it. Here Jehaziel must have dwelt. And here may we all dwell. There is room for us all. But let us remember that it is not the man who is near to God who is most honored, but the man nearest to God.

XXVI.

WHY WEEPEST THOU?

THE caption of this chapter was the first utterance of Christ after His resurrection. Of all things which he might have said, perhaps no more beautiful, blessed, needful, and significant speech could have been made by Him to His sorrowing disciples, and, beyond them, to the struggling, battling Church in all ages, and even to the sinful world itself. Since Christ died and rose again, it may well be asked, why should any one weep?

The question comes to the penitent, Why weepest thou?

Has not Christ died and paid the debt that you owe to an offended God and violated law? If He has, why not burst forth into rejoicing and singing, with the heaven-declared statement that Jesus has suffered for all, that He died for the ungodly, that no one might perish, but all have eternal life?

Every community and Church is familiar with a character who might well be called "the chronic mourner." These persons come to the altar at every meeting and at every call. They will not be comforted, seem unable to get relief, and certainly fail to receive the assurance they wish to possess.

In a certain city, lately, I was speaking to one of this class. She was a woman of seventy years of age. When I tried to bring her help and comfort, she contemplated me silently for a few moments, and said with a melodramatic air, "My brother, I have been a mourner for fifty-two years."

If she intended to astonish me, she succeeded perfectly. For a full minute I said nothing, as I looked upon this living monument of unbelief, this individual who had persisted in grieving over her sins for a half-century, as though Christ had never died and paid the full obligation she owed to Heaven in regard to the transgressions of the past. I even detected an accent of pride in the statement that she was a mourner of such long standing. She was no ordinary penitent. She had made a science out of spiritual grieving. She had been so satisfied with the words that they were blessed who mourned, that she refused to come to the other part of the sentence, "they shall be comforted." She knew nothing of that. She was a mourner, called herself one, when in the sight of God she was an unbeliever.

Is it not strange that people who will not look to Christ for pardon after He died for all sins, can not be made to see that in this fixed mental attitude they make Christ to die in vain, utterly contradict God's own Word, and discourage hundreds who would otherwise come to Christ and be delivered and blessed?

Again, the words apply to those who grieve over the presence of inbred sin.

While we do not have to repent over the existence of this principle, we can lament the fact of its being in us, and should go promptly to Christ for its destruction and removal.

After its discovery, to sit down and sorrow over the dark inheritance and fail to come to Christ with it, is to repeat the folly of the ordinary transgressor who will not let the Son of God save him.

To those of us who have gone within the veil, and exercised the second distinct faith for heart-cleansing or the sanctification of the soul, the days and weeks of protracted mourning and seeking by some, without the obtainment of the blessing is simply astounding. The blood has been shed outside the gate to sanctify the people; why weepest thou? Let us go forth at once to Him without the camp, bearing His reproach, and obtain the unspeakable grace.

We once saw a lady receive the blessing after a most faithful seeking for it for a few hours. She had to leave the meeting that night at ten o'clock on the cars in company with a lady friend. She was fairly electrified with her new possession, and the way into the Holiest being all plain to her, she bent over her friend who was at the altar, and who was weeping and grieving without securing what she desired, and exclaimed, while laughing and crying over her and clapping her on the shoulders, "Jennie, darling, make haste and get the blessing; the train will be here in fifteen minutes."

Quite a number around the altar smiled at the speech, but others saw deeper into the words, and to them it was a paraphrase of what Christ had long ago uttered, "Why weepest thou?"

When Christians refuse to thus cast themselves on the atoning sacrifice, it can readily be seen what a paralysis they occasion to the faith of others who are not spiritually strong to begin with, or are less exalted in social and ecclesiastical planes. So we have seen the slowness of a preacher in obtaining sanctification throw the entire Church back. Their eyes were on him as a kind of example, and as he did not sweep into the Holiest, they reasoned very naturally that there would be no need for them to try, and that there was no hope or prospect for them. O! that all seekers in pulpit and pew would look to Calvary, and behold the blood which cleanseth from all sin! O! that the voice of Christ could be heard by these sad, discouraged followers of His, whose highest conception of the Son of God in redemption is the suppression of the carnal mind, the keeping of the Old Man in a kind of subjection!

"Why weepest thou?" Is Christ not able to do exceeding abundantly for you above all that you can ask or think? Did he not say, "All things are possible to him that believeth," and "According to your faith so shall it be unto you?"

Still again the words apply to the bereaved.

How perfectly helpless all of us have been made to feel in a place and at an hour when Death has entered and taken away the light of the home! At such a time we feel the vanity of human consolation, the nothingness of human strength.

Once as a pastor we stood in the midst of a family who were grouped around the deathbed of a lovely daughter just grown, and now breathing her last. We shall never forget the affecting silence of those moments. No one spoke, but tears fell swiftly down every face. Each tired, heavy sigh from the pillow was feared to be the last breath, and when finally the physician, whose eyes were steadily fixed on the dying girl, looked up with a sad face and said quietly, "It is all over," I immediately called all to their knees around the bed, and in the midst of choking sobs, commended the grief-stricken family to Him who once died Himself and rose again, and who said that at His voice all that are in their graves shall come forth into everlasting life.

Mary in tears at the Savior's tomb is a picture which appeals to every heart. Here was an attitude, a burden, a sorrow known to us all. Then comes the footfall of Christ. His eye rests on the drooping figure, and His loving voice falls upon her ear—"Woman, why weepest thou?"

How quickly the tearstained face was raised; how it flashed and glowed with joy, we all can easily imagine, when in another moment, with an additional word from His lips, she saw it was Jesus. He had broken the bands of Death. The grave could not hold Him. He had come back to tell the grieving world of His victory, and that as He had raised Himself from the tomb, even so He would resurrect all who believe on Him.

Since that marvelous and blessed return, and since the words, "I am the resurrection and the life," how can there be inconsolable sorrow at the side of the deathbed, and by the margin of the grave?

"Thy brother shall rise again," said the Savior to the sisters of Bethany. And we have only to change the word brother to father, mother, husband, wife, sister, son, and daughter, to make them sound like sweetest music to every grieving, bereaved heart around the world. No wonder He said, "Why weepest thou?"

Once more, the words apply to the heart and life which has been wounded and injured by human tongues and influence.

Not only opposition and persecution have come, but lower, sadder still, misrepresentation, detraction, and slander are hurled like javelins and boomerangs at the servant of God. No office or position, and no religious experience or life of usefulness, is sufficient to protect one here.

The added pain is that oftentimes the blow is struck, not by a worldly hand, but by one who went with you to the house of God in company. We have seen some gentle Christian natures sink, completely crushed, under this peculiar form of malevolence.

Still we say, "Why weepest thou?" Why should we grieve hopelessly as though some strange thing had happened? Was not Christ slandered? Were not the disciples vilified? Was not Wesley accused of having broken all the commandments? And are we to expect better treatment than they received?

Again, has not Christ promised deliverance to us from this and every other evil? Does not the Bible say that all things work together for good to them that love God? Then, "Why weepest thou?"

Paul said, "None of these things move me;" and we should say the same, and go right on in God's service.

As for general misrepresentation, there are few revival-meetings in which every true evangelist does not see the funeral and burial of various kinds of false reports. We have nothing to do but discharge our duty, and "wait on the Lord," and the Bible says He will bring it to pass. He will deliver us from all our enemies, and cause us to inherit the land.

How many Christians worry needlessly in regard to these things! Some workers at times feel half-paralyzed, heartsick, and tempted to give up their labor for Christ and souls. My advice to them is to hold on, hold in, hold up, and hold out.

If a lie is told upon you, make no answer, but wait on the Lord, be of good courage, and "weep not." If a misrepresentation is circulated about your work, methods, family, or Christian life, and a thick door seems to be shut and locked in your face, do not think of opening it yourself. Do not lose time and energy in trying to prize it off its hinges or blowing it up with dynamite. Wait on the Lord, weep not, be patient, and suddenly it will open—and God will do the opening.

Your coat may be bespattered with the mud of human hate, detraction, or misconception. Mr. Spurgeon says, do not wipe it off at once, for that will simply smear it and make matters worse. Be patient, he said, and let it dry; by and by it will drop off of itself.

He will take care of the mud-flinger, the mud-flinging, the mud, and especially the coat and the man flung at. He, with His own touch, will brush off the mire, and show that it did not come from a fall of the man, but was cast upon him by the hand of an enemy. "Wait," I say, "on the Lord." In a word, "Why weepest thou?"

XXVII.

HOLY JOY.

MUCH has been said and written against what is called emotional or demonstrative religion. A great deal of sage advice and warning is given to people who are filled with the Spirit in such expressions as "Talking one's self empty," "Living one's religion," "Best proof of being well is walking around," and "Thunder kills nobody."

We are not in this chapter championing what has been scornfully dubbed "mere noise," although we cheerfully confess that we have not the slightest objection to the commotion and stir made by people who are genuinely filled with the Holy Ghost. We, in fact, like it. We have been heard and seen in these lines ourselves repeatedly by friend and foe; our comfort, meanwhile, being that, according to the second chapter of Acts, there was anything but a quiet time on the morning of Pentecost with the disciples; and John is our authority for saying that there was silence in heaven only for the space of a half-hour; after that, he heard the noise of a great multitude shouting and praising God, and it sounded like the voice of mighty thunders and the roar of many waters.

And yet, with all this, we are not contending for noise and what is called "fuss." We have listened to some which we wished that we had not heard. And yet the Church has not suffered as much in this way as it has with a graveyard quiet and deadness.

We are speaking in this connection of an inward condition and life, far back from the lips, in the heart, and that expresses itself in more ways than one; sometimes, indeed, with words; but sometimes being voiceless, but felt always as a penetrating, melting influence as powerful as any word or deed.

It is a peculiar joy we are writing about. Not the ecstasy of one of those many refreshings, anointings, and comfortings that come to the child of God, and as certainly leak out in a few minutes or hours. Nor is it the result of regeneration, but of the baptism with the Holy Ghost. It is not the gladness of the New Birth, but that strange rapture which comes from spiritual crucifixion and death.

There is a Divine work in the soul which introduces the Christian into the realm of joy as certainly as justification and regeneration brought him into the spiritual province of peace. "Being justified by faith, we have peace with God through our Lord Jesus Christ. By whom, *also*, we have access by faith into this grace, wherein we stand and rejoice."

He who will faithfully regard the spiritual multiplicands and multipliers of the Upper Room, and the ten days of faithful waiting and importunate praying, will beyond every shadow of doubt obtain the product of a full, steadfast, delicious, satisfying joy to abide in the soul.

Not all have it; for not all are true to God's arithmetic. There is trifling either with the multiplier or the multiplicand of consecration and faith. The fullness of waiting is not observed, the fervor and force of prayer is neglected; and so they "come short," as the apostle says, of the great blessing. The cold face, lackluster eye, hard facial lines, and lack of spiritual spring and buoyancy, plainly indicate the failure to the observant, fire-baptized disciple. For some reason best known to themselves and God, they have not obtained that blessed result called the Secret of the Lord, and the Mystery of the Gospel. They can grasp the idea of peace and occasional overflowings of spiritual gladness; but the fact of a constant, abiding, upspringing joy in the soul is beyond their comprehension.

The holy joy we speak of arises from a sense of conscious cleanness, sweet submissiveness to God's will, and the perpetual presence of Christ in the soul. With this is felt the nestling of a perfect love in the heart and the blessed throbbings of spiritual power.

Who wonders, then, at the presence of a perennial gladness and sunshininess in such a heart? The marvel would be if, after such a work, there would be no such resultant condition.

The outward manifestation of this inner joy is unmistakable. It may differ somewhat, according to circumstances and temperament; but with all that, there are signs of this deeper salvation in those who possess it that are not to be beheld in the regenerated man, no matter how true and faithful he may be.

One mark is a peculiar brightness of the face. Another is a smiling expression. A third is a restful look about the eyes, brow, lips, and, indeed, all the lines of the face. A fourth sign is recognized in the voice, in an indescribable ring and accent which comes from the heart and goes to the heart. A fifth is a certain instinctive and instantaneous responsiveness of the soul to all that is read and preached from God's Word on this hidden life. A sixth is a spring and buoyancy of the spirit which makes it difficult at times to refrain from what might be called physical demonstrativeness. A seventh is the language of praise that becomes as natural as the breathing of a healthy lung. Just as the sin-burdened heart has words of complaint, fault-finding, gloom, and despair, so the blood-washed and fire-baptized soul has a language that describes and declares its own restfulness, contentedness, gladness, and blessedness in a constantly indwelling Christ.

If we single out any one of the above marks just mentioned, and study their effect on the world around us, we will have at once furnished the most urgent motives as Christians for seeking to enter upon such a spiritual life.

Think of the power of a restful face as it is seen daily unchanged in the midst of the varying circumstances of life!

Such a sweet, glad countenance, that of an elderly woman, who had troubles and sorrows enough to have crushed a giant, created deep convictions in all who beheld her. The patient, kindly smile she turned on her home-circle, friends, and acquaintances, in spite of her life-burdens, was a call in itself to high regions of Christian living that reached a loftier note to the spiritual ear than the trumpet-blast which sounds loud and clear from Mt. Sinai.

As for the language of praise so familiar to those who are deeply and genuinely sanctified, the moral effect is even more powerful. It bubbles up from a filled and overflowing heart. Language is felt to be a relief. The lip and tongue are like channels conveying away some of the fullness of the abundantly satisfied soul. Oftentimes the quietly uttered "Praise the

Lord," "Hallelujah," "Glory," "Bless the Lord," is spoken in perfect unconsciousness of human auditors. Men hear the words with wonder. Various may be the opinions of the listeners; but there is conviction in the expressions for them all.

So Paul and Silas praised God in the dungeon, and it brought about a revival. No astonishment would have been felt by the prisoners in the outer prison over the language of complaint and lamentation. They were accustomed to that. But when two men in the inner prison, all bloody with a dreadful scourging, and with feet stuck in the stocks, sang and praised God at midnight, so that Nature itself bore witness to the moral grandeur of the occurrence, both jailer and prisoners alike were brought down in an awful fear and bitter repentance before God.

The rejoicing and praises of the martyrs as they were crucified, torn to pieces by wild animals, or slowly burned to death at the stake, did more to spread Christianity than all the eloquent sermons ever preached. A singing, shouting, praising Christian sank finally into a heap of ashes; but thousands of people returned home from the awful spectacle beating their breasts and convicted to their hearts. Out of this number many would turn to Christ and be saved. That voice of praise and rejoicing going up from the curling smoke and crackling flames was a divine argument, a heavenly proof, a voice from the sky itself that could not be answered, doubted, or gainsaid. And so the blood of the martyrs became the seed of the Church.

We knew a preacher who was hurled from a large church and handsome salary for preaching sanctification as a direct, instantaneous work of Christ in the soul of the believer. Instead of complaining, he went to the man who had cast him out, and with a joy that he could not keep out of face or voice said, "I expect to do the best work of my life this year." The happy look and joyful spirit and speech of the victim, without any intention upon his part, troubled the man he spoke to far more than a volume of reproaches and complaints. In fact, he talked about it for months, and said he could not forget it, or get over it.

Again, if the joy should declare itself in the action of the body, there is peculiar convicting power even in that manifestation.

We would not indorse all the bodily exercise we have seen. Some "profiteth little," and some is overdone, and does harm rather than good. But there have been physical manifestations of the inner joy, both in pulpit and pew, upon which the Holy Ghost, who had already inspired the movement, now fell again with approving power.

The sight of David leaping before the ark seemed to have aroused but one harsh critic, and that was Michal, the wife of the rejoicing man. But it must be remembered that she was some distance off, and was looking through a window, while David was close to the ark. He was coming up the road with the Holy Oracles, and in good religious company. A great deal depends upon being in the procession.

Sometimes cool-blooded Christians in the audience have wondered at something they beheld in the demonstrative way in the pulpit. They failed to see how it could have been done. The explanation is that they were looking through the window, and labored under the additional disadvantage of spiritual distance. The man in the pulpit saw a glory they could not see, and heard the rolling of the wheels which is to bring up the ark to Jerusalem.

A preacher was watching another at a camp-meeting. He studied his pulpit movements closely. He saw him give a leap at a climactic point in the discourse. The solemn comment of the observer was, "that it had cost the speaker a great deal to be able to do what he had done that day." The man's eyes filled when he heard the true discriminating words. He, above all men, knew for himself "that with a great price he had obtained this freedom." One other thing he knew, and that was that he never let the great indwelling joy overflow in an irresistible manner by way of the body rather than the tongue; but the Holy Ghost used it as an arrow to pierce men and women with conviction. It is true that the scoffer might be present; but so they were at Pentecost; yet while some laughed and doubted that day, many beat their breasts, and said, "What must we do?"

Finally this joy is our strength. The Bible says so: "The joy of the Lord is your strength."

More and more the writer is convinced that it is not human eloquence, logic, or wisdom that is to win the day; that it is not ecclesiastical pomp, ceremony, or power which will vanquish the enemies of God; that it is not scholarship, culture, position, reputation, influence, high places, and offices that constitute the strength of the Church. We will never conquer with these things and by these methods. Our strength is the joy of the Lord; our invincibility will be found in being filled with the Holy Ghost.

Men and women drunk on the wine of the Kingdom, intoxicated with the love of God, and whose faces are shining with a rapture not born of earth, but sent down from heaven, will be not only a spectacle but an actual spiritual force, under which the people will be compelled to go down before God. It did so at Pentecost, has done so often since, and will do so again to the end of time.

It rests with the Church to say how long the nations shall stay away from Christ, and the world lie in wickedness.

The victory will never come with the use of carnal weapons, or by legislation, or by fighting symptoms, or by all the proprieties, moralities, and orthodoxies of the Church and Christian life. The devil does not care how proper and orthodox we are, provided we do not get the Holy Ghost. And the triumph will never be obtained by quietness, peacefulness, and peaceableness. It will never be brought to pass by the forces which lie in justification and regeneration, and the faithful, excellent lives of good people.

The Church will have to get drunk on joy. There must be an intoxication of spirit, as the body is with wine. There must be a bubbling gladness in the heart; an overflowing of a sweet, holy rapture, that can not be restrained, but will rush into every open channel of privilege, opportunity, and duty, and with sunlit face, shining eyes, liberated tongues, praising lips, and flying bodies carry the food, light, comfort, and treasures of the gospel to the starving, benighted, broken-hearted, and bankrupted nations of the earth.

Who is it that sneers at an emotional, demonstrative religion, when, according to the Bible, two-thirds of it is feeling? Look and see—"The kingdom of heaven is righteousness, peace, and joy in the Holy Ghost."

Lately a convention of preachers was called in Texas to ask one another what was the matter with the Church, and why there is such a dearth of revivals. Our reply would have been, let the Church seek for the baptism with the Holy Ghost, be fired and filled with this holy joy, and salvation will roll over the land like a deluge.

The Lord's command to his people on the eve of a great battle was not to take sword or spear, but to go forth with harps, singing and praising the beauty of holiness, and that all would be well. The reader has only to turn to the Old Testament to read the account of the marvelous victory which followed, when the people sang, rejoiced, and praised God, and without using a weapon saw the Almighty mow their enemies down before their eyes.

May we take the lesson to heart, and at once seek and obtain the experience which places the harp in the hand, the song in the heart, the light in the face, the praise on the lips, and the leap to the feet, and thereafter see as stupendous victories for God and His Truth as were ever beheld in the centuries and ages that are gone!

XXVIII.

"LOOKING UNTO JESUS."

SALVATION is brought to the soul by looking to the crucified Son of God. It was taught in symbol before the tragedy of Calvary took place. The Jews, when bitten by fiery serpents, were told to look to a Brazen Serpent uplifted on a pole. If, instead, they looked at the reptile which stung them, or at the bitten place, or at Moses, or at the Tabernacle, they all died. But whosoever looked upon the uplifted Brazen Serpent lived. It mattered not how far the man was gone, or how many reptiles had poisoned him; it mattered not if friends had to hold up his head and with merciful finger lift up the drooping eyelid; the instant the eye fell upon the Serpent on the Pole the man felt a great rush of life in him, leaped to his feet, and became sound and whole.

Christ Himself declared that He was the fulfillment of this remarkable type; that He would be lifted up on the cross, that "whosoever believeth on Him should not perish, but have eternal life." Salvation for a look to Jesus.

Of course, the world wonders and stumbles over this condition of pardon, men failing to see the justice involved, the love that inspired, and the profound wisdom which permeated the whole infinite act and sacrifice. They especially stagger over the simple requirement of a look to be saved. The spiritual thinker sees far deeper, and knows that the looking to means also a looking from. He who looks to Jesus is doing a marvelous thing in the spiritual life. Just as the eye was turned from crawling reptiles and festering wounds, from self and surrounding friends, from the great leader Moses, and the beautiful Tabernacle, and was fastened on a serpent of brass hanging on a pole, and all this done at the command of God, so the sinner looks away from the devil and his own sin-poisoned soul, from all hope of self and human strength, looks beyond the preachers, gazes higher than the Church, and, fastening his eyes upon the Crucified One, cries,

> "In my hand no price I bring,
> Simply to thy cross I cling,"

and is instantly filled with salvation, sweet, restful, and blessed, and knows he has eternal life. It was a look from earth to heaven, from men to God, from sin to Christ, and God rewarded it with an instantaneous pardon and glorious rush of spiritual life into the soul.

But the necessity of looking unto Jesus is not

ended by regeneration. Paul was not addressing sinners in pursuit of forgiveness, but Christians in a race for heaven. Even then, in such a blessed life, he says, there must be a steady looking unto Jesus.

Indeed, the expression is used after every weight, and "the sin which doth so easily beset" has been laid aside. Here is a spiritual state which plainly indicates that the second great look has been cast upon Him who has been made unto us, not only righteousness or pardon, but sanctification. There is a look to Christ on Mount Calvary, and there is a second waiting and look to Him on Mount Zion. The cross brings one experience, the Upper Room another. One is life, the other power. One is a birth, the other a baptism. One brings peace, the other purity. Both come from looking to Jesus. They can come in no other way; the Bible and life prove it.

And yet after this, when the "weights" are laid aside, and "the sin which doth so easily beset" is gone, and we are running toward the goal of glory, the look to Jesus must be kept up. Here is where the trouble begins with many. Here is the cause of weakness, hesitation, and failure in the Christian life—the eyes have been more or less turned from Jesus. For several reasons we are to cast the steady, continued look upon Christ.

One is for constant cleansing.

We do not mean that inbred sin is left in the heart, or that sin is being committed in the life; but we refer to a blissful experience in which the soul is continually thrilled with the consciousness of being kept clean.

A man who does not know this secret of the Lord said once to the writer, "If the heart has to be cleansed all the while, then it must be defiled all the while." My reply to him was, "Yes, just about as unclean as a clean rock on clean white sand, with the clear water of a brook flowing over it all the time." He saw the picture and the idea, and was silent.

By a steady look to Jesus we can keep under the Blood, and feel every second its cleansing power as it flows over the soul. We fail to see the necessity of sin, while rejoicing at the same time in the delightful realization of perpetual whiteness and purity.

Again we must look to Jesus for perfect conformity to Him in all things.

We may have pardoned and purified hearts, and yet the outward life is left with all its manifold features of speech and act, looks, tones, gestures, bearing, manners, and scores of other things that are not necessarily sinful, but need to be corrected and changed. Sanctification means great light, but not all light, as some would make it. It means perfect love; but not a perfect head by any manner of means. It means that the sin principle is out of the soul; but does not mean that we can not grow in grace within, or be improved in our ways and manners without.

The thing to do is to look to Jesus, with the question, What would He say, and What would He do under the circumstances which surround us? Nor should we be discouraged in not obtaining all the light at once. We are to keep looking, and blessed will be the result to ourselves, and marked will be the improvement in the eyes of those who are proper judges of spiritual things.

A mechanic or contractor bending over the plans of the building which is being erected, should be both a rebuke and inspiration to us.

A musician with his eyes on the notes of a piece of music, making the fingers to fall just when and just how the printed sheet before him directs, and going over and over it until the rendering agrees with the original; such a sight is a sermon in itself, and is enough to make every careless Christian ashamed of himself, and arouse him to greater faithfulness and Christlikeness.

Christ is our plan, our example and model; and so the eyes of the soul should be fixed steadfastly upon Him, that the life might be made to agree in all things possible with Him. Men took knowledge of the disciples, that they had been with Jesus. So they can and will note us, if we are Christlike.

Christ has brought a marvelous soul harmony into the world. Souls are being thrilled, melted, and drawn to God by it. We are to study the notes that fell from His lips and life in Bethlehem, Bethany, and Jerusalem, in Judea and Galilee, in Gethsemane and Calvary, and reproduce the melody. When we, with the Gospel before us, and the Holy Spirit within us, strike the right chords and utter the right note, people around us both feel and know it. When we strike a false or discordant note, they also know it.

All of us can recall times when we suffered excruciating pain of a mental character in having to listen to incorrect playing, and what is called flat or falsetto singing. The ear, nerve, mind, and heart all partook together of the misery. Even more painful is the fact of un-Christlikeness in the words, manner, spirit, and deeds of a Christian. The appearance of spiritual vanity and pride, of irritability and uncharitableness, of faultfinding and tattling, of arrogance, selfishness, and bitterness, even if only for a moment, sends a pang through the soul. It was so unlike the other part of the life song, it was so different from the notes given by Christ in the Four Gospels, it had such a falsetto ring, that all looked up pained, and felt, even if they said nothing, that the music of Bethany and Galilee had not been followed.

Our only hope is to keep the eyes fixed on Jesus. This is our duty and our privilege. If we are faithful here, we will not only realize blessedness within, but discover we have power without. Men will want us to bring them to Him who created such melody of heart and harmony in life within us. And we will bring them.

Still again, we must look to Jesus for guidance.

With all the power of a splendid intellect, and the knowledge which experience brings, yet the child of God is still under the necessity of being Divinely led and directed in the daily steps of life. This need springs from the fact of our ignorance concerning God's plans, our inability to understand people, and our lack of power to read the future, and know what is best for us to do.

The Lord has promised to lead the soul which will faithfully, patiently, and obediently look to and follow Him. He will guide, He says, with His Word, His Spirit, and His eye. All these three are mentioned in the Scripture, and show different degrees of nearness upon the part of the soul to God. There is an undoubted advancement from the "Word" to the "eye." Just as well-trained servants get so that they do not need to be spoken to at the table, but a glance will show them what is wanted; so the Christian first held in and held back, and only able to go by explicit statements, comes at last to understand the movements of the Holy Spirit upon the soul, and finally walks certainly and triumphantly amid a whirl of duties, conflicts, and perils, guided by the looks of Christ.

He has promised to guide us in all things, and lead us into all truth. The leading will not be violent, but very gentle; it will be a still, small voice rather than a thunder-clap; it will be recognized as a drawing rather than a driving; but it will be unmistakable to the faithful, devoted man of God, and will always bring one into realms of spiritual rest and assurance.

A good thing to do, when duties seem to conflict, the road forks, and it is difficult to tell which of two ways to take, is to wait on the Savior in prayer, and ask Him to shine on the path He would have us tread, making it sweetly attractive to the soul, and at the same time put a kind of fog upon the other and cause it to have a forbidding appearance. Christ will do it. We are convinced that He will lead us in every step of life; in business, pleasure, marriage, Church relations, and all, if we fix our eyes upon Him, and patiently wait for light and direction.

Anna Shipton tells us in one of her books how

Christ allowed her to turn aside from her regular work to rest a few days in an Italian town, and write on one of her forthcoming volumes. She became so absorbed that she went beyond the number of days she first asked for, and suddenly discovered that the flying pen had lost its power, and that her brain had ceased to create. She was wondering about it one night while wakeful in bed, when a large bird, blown by the storm from the mountains, gave a scream near her window-shutters, which sounded like the word "Direct." Yes, said the convicted woman, that is just what I want, and have failed to ask for—direction from Christ, and on her knees in another minute came the impression she must leave the town. The next day, while speeding on the train, with a happy feeling of being in the line of duty, she led a man to God on the cars, which work of grace led to a still greater gospel work in another town.

Once more we must look to Jesus for comfort.

We continually need it in such a world as this. The whole race in its sinfulness and heart-brokenness wants consolation for that matter. But deeper still is the need of the Christian, who, hated by hell, cast off by the world, and misunderstood by friends, is certainly bereaved, indeed, if he has not heaven to turn to for consolation.

But this comfort is to be received and enjoyed,

and so deep and satisfying is it that one possessing such a blessing can rejoice in the sorest tribulations of earth and time.

A distinguishing title of the Holy Ghost is the Comforter. Christ said He would send Him into the world, knowing the paramount need for Him. The Savior also said, "I will not leave you comfortless; I will come to you."

Different from anointing for special service, dissimilar to sudden influxes of energy and power to proclaim the Word or make some notable stand for duty, is the sweet comfort with which Christ can fill the soul. Bringing as it does a perfect melting of the soul, tenderness of spirit, gladness in loneliness, contentedness to live, suffer, or die, to be or do anything for Jesus—it is an experience so unearthly, so holy, so heavenly, as to be beyond the power of verbal description. Jesus in some way takes the tired, grieved, hurt, lonely soul in His arms and comforts it.

We once heard a prominent preacher say, with the tears running down his face, that since his mother had died he had found a place where he could go and cry out all his troubles and get perfect comfort, and that place was the lap of Jesus.

Once at a camp-meeting I saw a business man, who had been through great griefs and trials, suddenly obtain the comfort which Christ loves to bestow, while sitting disconsolately behind a large wooden column in the Tabernacle. The transformation was amazing! Who, when in sadness and loneliness, does not love a dear one to hunt them up, and with hand and voice cheer and heal the aching heart? So Jesus found His grieving servant behind the pillar, and putting His arms around him, comforted him. O, how the man wept! The fountains of the deep were broken up, his form shook under the emotion which filled him, while his face shone with the light and peace and holy calm of heaven.

I have seen a father rough to his child, and beheld the weeping little fellow go to his mother, who, with soothing words, tender kiss, and embrace, and some promise of the morrow, would cause the child to completely forget his sorrow. The little, tear-stained face would be turned up gleefully to hers, the tongue talk happily about other things, and the only sign left of the other experience would be an occasional catch in his breath, the last sighs of the almost spent breast storm. And so have I seen God's child struck by the world and deeply hurt. Then I have beheld him go to Jesus and look up to Him, and at once get such calm of mind, comfort of heart, and forgetfulness of what had been said and done to him, that the face glowed like a seraph, and any one could see that he had been caught away from the strife of tongues, the pride and wrath of man, and was hidden in the secret place of the Most High.

We all know what it is to seek human comfort and fail to find it when the heart is fairly breaking for sympathy. Some of us know what it is to lie awake at night with a great sorrow, or walk through the house while all are quietly sleeping, and have to wrestle alone with the trouble. The peaceful sleeping of the household intensifies the loneliness, and adds to the pang. You walk out on the street, and the whole town is asleep. Everybody is at rest but yourself. By and by you come back and sit on the steps of your own house, heartsick and solitary under the stars. How far away they seem! Suddenly it occurs to you to look to Jesus, and instantly you are filled with a holy peace and comfort, which would make words bend and break to describe. The tortured heart is at rest, the fever has been banished from the spirit, Jesus has come to comfort you! He had been waiting all along for His follower to look up to Him. He had not been asleep like the household and town, for His eyelids never slumber. As I have heard my mother, now in heaven, sing when I was a child,

> "Though the night be dark and dreary,
> Darkness can not hide from Thee;
> Thou art He, who never weary,
> Watcheth where Thy people be."

Finally, we look to Jesus for reward.

Beyond the approval of conscience, the smile of God, and the blessedness of godly living, we are told by the Bible not to look for our recompense as Christians in this life from men.

The Scripture informs us that the world will hate us; that if we live godly in Christ Jesus we shall suffer persecution; that men will say all manner of evil against us; that our good will be evil spoken of; and we will be as strangers and pilgrims in the earth.

More than this, we learn that the closer we live to God, the less will we be understood; while enmity will be encountered, not only from the world, but in the Church. We will be cast out of the synagogue, and, sadder still, our foes will be they of our own household. The circles to which we would naturally go for appreciative sympathy and reward are seen, under these words, to be steadily lessening and narrowing all the time.

To be in a spiritual experience above others, is to be a mystery to them; and not to be comprehended in matters of grace and religion, has been equivalent to the dungeon, stake, and headsman's axe in the past, and means anything but an easy time in the present.

The price which Madam Guyon had to pay for

holiness of heart was her own beautiful head laid on the block of the executioner. The cost to John Wesley was mobs, slander, and constant persecution. While to-day a man who would enter the Holy of Holies in the Christian life, must lay down his reputation at the door, and consent to be ridiculed by the world, discounted and struck at by the Church, misunderstood by his own household, and walk a lonely path to heaven.

In view of these things, the man who would look for reward for his faith and labor from sinners, and even Christians, is worse than a fool, and doomed to bitter disappointment.

Tell them your hardships and trials for the Truth, and some few will listen the first time, but grow restless under a second recital, and yawn and count you a bore at the third.

But what we can not find in men, we can obtain in Christ. He never turns a deaf ear to our words, or sends us away empty. He rewards both here and hereafter. He gives the overflowing cup, the anointed head, and a table spread in the presence of our enemies even in this world, as a kind of hint and type of the great unseen eternal reward. Our soul delighting itself as with marrow and fatness, our spirit kept like a watered garden, songs in the night, praises in the dungeon, companionship in the wilderness, opening heavens on Patmos, and Christ looking us up when we are cast out from the councils and company of the synagogue, is part of Christ's blessed recompense in this world.

As for the reward at the last day, what pen can describe, or brush depict, or tongue declare the things which God has prepared for them who love Him? It is enough to stagger the imagination, overwhelm the mind, and yet electrify the soul, and make men leap for joy, to read expressions that are dropped here and there in the Bible, about thrones, crowns, kingdoms, glorious bodies, exceeding and eternal weights of glory; and yet realize that these wonderful terms are but hints in themselves of the reward which Christ has promised to all who will be faithful to Him unto the end.

It is natural to look to men, and especially to friends and kindred, for recompense and reward in the spiritual life; but it is a mistake to do so for all that, and sooner or later we find it out. People are too selfish, or busy, or burdened with their own toils and sorrows, to give the time to the consideration and proper treatment of cases which appeal to them for recognition and help. It is a bitter piece of knowledge to obtain, but a profitable experience when it comes, and happy is the man who does not sour in learning it.

We had best look to Jesus. We will not be disappointed there. We will get all that the heart craves and the life deserves from His faithful, loving, pitiful hand.

An old preacher was struck down suddenly with the pangs of approaching death. For the first few moments he was bewildered with the confusion and excitement of his family in the room, the fainting sensations of the body, and the dimness which came upon his sight. With a trembling, piteous voice, he exclaimed, "Where is Jesus, my old, true, life-long friend?" Then with a sudden burst of sunshine in his face he said, with a deep, contented sigh, "Ah! here He is—and now it is all right."

If the writer, before drawing his last breath and sinking into the grave, was allowed to write or speak but three words to the world or Church, to old or young, to sinner or saint, to the justified or sanctified, those three words should be, "Look to Jesus."

Pentecostal Light,

By REV. A. M. HILLS.

---

101 Large Pages. Price in Cloth, 50 Cents. In Paper Cover, 10 Cents.

THIS BOOK TREATS OF:

"Praying for the Spirit. Filled with the Spirit. Grieve not the Spirit."

IT HAS HAD A CIRCULATION OF OVER THREE THOUSAND IN TWELVE MONTHS.

Rev. S. T. Morris, of Calumet, Mich., writes:
"Pentecostal Light is a work of power, and should be in the hands of every believer in America. It is rightly named, and you have my special thanks for writing it."
"The last chapter alone is worth its price."
"Effective medicine for worldliness among professors.

Address M. W. KNAPP, Revivalist Office,

CINCINNATI, OHIO.

Tears and Triumphs

~No. 2.~

By L. L. PICKETT and M. W. KNAPP.

One of the Best Song Books for the Price Ever Issued.

It is Pentecostal, Evangelical, Loyal.

It is printed in round and shaped notes, contains a Topical Index, an Index of Choruses, and single songs worth more than its price.

It contains the merits intensified which pushed the sale of "Tears and Triumphs" No. 1 in so short a time to

.. **OVER 100,000 COPIES** ..

One firm ordered 2,000 before the book appeared. Others are buying by the hundred and thousand. From the

NIAGARA OF PRAISE

which it is receiving the following few drops have been selected:

Western Christian Advocate, Cincinnati.—"Will be greatly appreciated by lovers of inspiring song in Sunday-school and revival work."

Rev. J. C. Johnson.—"I had four dozen yesterday and sold them in a few minutes. Its soul-stirring songs take with all denominations."

A Teacher and Composer orders 200 and writes: "I do not hesitate to pronounce it one of the best books for the purpose intended now on the market; a marvel of completeness."

Evangelist D. B. Geruigan.—"We sold the last one of the song books, 150, before the meeting closed. It is a book for the people. They shout and cry as they sing. It is the best book I ever saw."

Mrs. O. C. McGarvey, Music Teacher.—"It is better adapted to revival meetings than any book we have ever seen. I consider it a collection of the most spiritual songs I have ever seen."

G. E. Kersey, Teacher and Musical Composer.—"It is the best new song book on the market for camp-meeting, revival, church and home."

W. M. Patty.—"Indeed, it is a triumph in the interest of holy song."

*** *It is adapted to Evangelistic Work, Camp-Meetings, Prayer and Praise Meetings, Sunday-schools and General Church Worship.*

Such men as Hoffman, Bryant, Sweney, Palmer, Ogden, Kirkpatrick, Kieffer, McIntosh, Tillman, Lincoln, Street, Black, T. L. Perkins, W. O. Perkins, Rev. J. E. Rankin, Gilmour and many others have assisted in making it.

☞ Try the following: Nos. 5, 6, 7, 32, 35, 56, 58, 60, 62, 63, 70, 76, 85, 91, 94, 116, 118, 121, 125, 132, 133, 147, 149, 154, 155, 163, 168, 179, 180, 187, 193, 195, 196, 199. If not pleased, return it and get your money back.

PRICES: Board, 25c. prepaid; $2.80 per doz. prepaid; $20 per 100 not prepaid. Muslin, 20c. prepaid; $2.25 per doz. prepaid; $16 per 100 not prepaid. Printed in round and shaped notes. State which you wish.

ORDER OF THIS OFFICE.

FOOD FOR LAMBS;

OR,

LEADING CHILDREN TO CHRIST.

BY A. M. HILLS,

Author of "Holiness and Power" and "Pentecostal Light."

Abridged Edition.

Price, 10 Cents; 16 for $1.00.

TABLE OF CONTENTS—Chapter I., Why God Calls Children Early; II., Same—Continued; III., Same—Continued; IV., Two Other Reasons Why God Calls Little Children to Remember Him and Seek Him; V., First Condition of Salvation—Repentance; VI., The Second Condition of Salvation—Faith; VII., The Third Condition of Salvation—Surrender of Self to God's Service; VIII. Coming to Christ.

Complete Edition.

Price, Cloth, 80 Cents; 4 Copies, $2.40.

TABLE OF CONTENTS—Chapter I., Why God Calls Children Early; II., Same—Continued; III., Same—Continued; IV., Two Other Reasons Why God Calls Little Children to Remember Him and Seek Him; V., First Condition of Salvation—Repentance; VI., The Second Condition of Salvation—Faith; VII., The Third Condition of Salvation—Surrender of Self to God's Service; VIII., Coming to Christ; IX., Ten Evidences of Conversion: X., Prayer; XI, The Bible; XII., Obedience; XIII., A Life of Love; XIV., A Life of Service; XV., Joining the Church; XVI., Religion Made Easy by the Holy Ghost.

This is an invaluable and timely Text-Book for training Children in the Home, Sunday-School and Day School.

No Parent or Teacher can Afford to be Without it.

Free from cant and adapted to believers of every name. It will help fasten truth in the child-mind as no other book we know.

The 80-cent Book and The Weekly Revivalist,
One Year, **$1.50.**

ORDER OF THIS OFFICE.

Burning Books
By Seth C. Rees,
The Quaker Author and Evangelist.

I. FIRE FROM HEAVEN.

Over 300 pages. Price, $1.00. If you appreciate celestial light and fire, you will be delighted with this book. Four copies, postpaid, for the price of three.

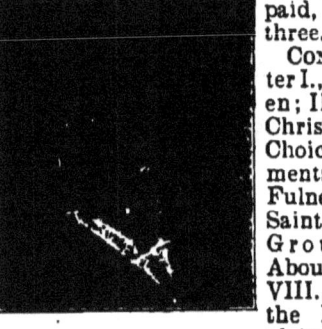

CONTENTS: Chapter I., Fire from Heaven; II., Established in Christ; III., God's Choice of Instruments; IV., Stephen's Fulness; V., The True Saint; VI., Rooted and Grounded; VII., Abounding Grace; VIII., The Secret of the Lord; IX., Exploits; X., A Larger Outlook; XI., Abundant Resources; XII., More Than Conquerors; XIII., This is That; XIV., The Holy Peace; XV., Call of Rebecca; XVI., Blessings in Disguise.

II. PENTECOSTAL CHURCH.

Like the Bible and the Life of Jesus, it combines the characteristics of the Lamb and the Lion, the Lily and the Lightning.

CONTENTS: Chapter I., Opening Words; II., The Ideal Pentecostal Church is Composed of Regenerated Souls; III., A Clean Church; IV., A Powerful Church; V., A Powerful Church—Continued; VI., A Witnessing Church; VII., Without Distinction as to Sex; VIII., A Liberal Church; IX., A Demonstrative Church; X., An Attractive Church—Draws the People Together; XI., Puts People Under Conviction; XII., Will Have Healthy Converts; XIII., A Joyful Church; XIV., A Unit; XV., The Power of the Lord is Present to Heal the Sick; XVI., A Missionary Church; XVII., Out of Bondage; XVIII., Entering into Canaan; XIX., The Land and Its Resources; XX., Samson; XXI., Power Above the Power of the Enemy; XXII., Compromise and Its Evil Effects; XXIII., Sermon; XXIV., The Author's Experience.

Price, 50 cents; four copies, postpaid, $1.50. Special rates by the quantity.

OLD CORN.

BY

DAVID B. UPDEGRAFF.

TABLE OF CONTENTS.

CHAPTER I, Old Corn; CHAPTER II, The Blood of Christ; CHAPTER III, Cleansing Through the Blood; CHAPTER IV, Consecration; CHAPTER V, The Baptism with the Holy Ghost; CHAPTER VI, Is Pentecost Repeated? CHAPTER VII, Power for Service; CHAPTER VIII, Mistakes of Simon Magus; CHAPTER IX, "Our Old Man;" CHAPER X, Crucified with Christ; CHAPTER XI, The World Crucified; CHAPTER XII, Steps in the Experience of the Apostles; CHAPTER XIII, Self-Purification; CHAPTER XIV, Unto Perfection; CHAPTER XV, A Good Conscience; CHAPTER XVI, Shall He Find Faith? CHAPTER XVII, Self-Preservation; CHAPTER XVIII, Antagonisms to Holiness; CHAPTER XIX, Spirituality *vs.* Ritualism; CHAPTER XX, Last Promise of Jesus; CHAPTER XXI, Divine Guidance; CHAPTER XXII, John the Baptist; CHAPTER XXIII, An Unexpected Decree: CHAPTER XXIV, Christ's Coming Premillennial; CHAPTER XXV, The Parousia; CHAPTER XXVI, Free from the Law; CHAPTER XXVII, Serving in "Newness" or "Oldness"—Which? CHAPTER XXVIII, Suffering and Glorification; CHAPTER XXIX, Salvation through Sanctification; CHAPTER XXX, The Parables; CHAPTER XXXI, Sin Not a Necessity; CHAPTER XXXII, Distinctions; CHAPTER XXXIII, Philosophy of Doubt; CHAPTER XXXIV, Negative Ritualism; CHAPTER XXXV, Trinity, the New Birth, etc.; CHAPTER XXXVI, Personal Testimony.

Price, $1.00; Four Copies, prepaid, $3.00.

It and THE REVIVALIST, weekly, one year, $1.75.

Send all orders to

M. W. KNAPP,
REVIVALIST OFFICE, CINCINNATI, OHIO.

Books by Byron J. Rees.

THE HEART CRY OF JESUS.

CLOTH, 40 CENTS.

HULDAH, THE PENTECOSTAL PROPHETESS.

Every sentence is compact and precious as beaten gold.—*The American Friend.*

CLOTH, 50 CENTS.

CHRISTLIKENESS AND OTHER PAPERS.

There is something in it for every one. If you want an uplifting and inspiration for a higher life, read this book.—*Christian Standard.*

PAPER, 25 CENTS.

The Set, Post-paid, $1.00.

WITH

The Weekly Revivalist, $1.80.

Address

M. W. KNAPP,

OFFICE OF THE REVIVALIST,

Cincinnati, O.   Providence, R. I.

www.ingramcontent.com/pod-product-compliance
Lightning Source LLC
Chambersburg PA
CBHW032109230426
43672CB00009B/1687